# The Fair Garden
# and
# the Swarm of Beasts

# The Fair Garden
# and
# the Swarm of Beasts

*The Library and the*
*Young Adult*

Reprint Edition

## MARGARET A. EDWARDS

*With a Foreword by Patty Campbell*

American Library Association
CHICAGO   1994   LONDON

*Edwards* 025.1

Bonnie Smothers, acquisitions editor

Composed by Publishing Services, Inc., Bettendorf, Iowa
in Palatino on Xyvision/Linotype L330

Insert printed on 70-pound Sterling Litho Gloss
Text printed on 50-pound Glatfelter, a pH-neutral stock,
and bound in 10-point C1S cover stock
by Braun-Brumfield, Inc.

The paper used in this publication meets the minimum requirements of American National Standard for Information Sciences—Permanence of Paper for Printed Library Materials, ANSI Z39.48–1984.

**Library of Congress Cataloging-in-Publication Data**

Edwards, Margaret A.
   The fair garden and the swarm of beasts : the library and the young adult / Margaret A. Edwards ; with a foreword by Patty Campbell.
      p.    cm.
   "Reprint ed."
   Includes index.
   ISBN 0-8389-0635-4
   1. Young adults' libraries—United States—Administration.
   2. Teenagers—United States—Books and reading.  I. Title.
Z718.5.E36   1994
025.1'97626—dc20                                                  94-14269

Printed in the United States of America.
98  97  96  95  94        5  4  3  2  1

BoT 20.00 (net)
2/13/95

# Contents

v

# Foreword

## by Patty Campbell

Margaret Alexander Edwards—a magic name to young adult librarians. An ardent, true believer in the goodness of reading and a passionate advocate for young people, she articulated the principles and practices of an entire profession, and inspired the convictions that give it vitality. Although she retired over thirty years ago and died in 1988, her presence is still very much among us, in the many librarians she trained and influenced, and in the book—*this* book—in which she laid out her ideas and explained how to put them into practice. When *School Library Journal* and the Young Adult Library Services Association of ALA established an award to honor the lifetime achievements of young adult authors, it seemed quite inevitable and appropriate that it be blessed with the magic name of Margaret Edwards.[1]

Yet this woman who has been called the patron saint of young adult librarianship was a beloved autocrat and a stubborn missionary who was saved from fanaticism by a sense of humor. She was a force to be reckoned with in the classroom, but her students remember her with lifelong gratitude. Her charismatic personality made her a powerful leader in the development of library services to teenagers, although sometimes over the resistance of her supervisors and colleagues. Astonishingly, her work with young people was done without the benefit of young adult literature, because she retired five years before the beginnings of the genre. Her one book, *The Fair Garden and the Swarm of Beasts*, is still regarded as the cornerstone of young adult librarianship, and although some of her highly personal philosophy would part company with contemporary ideas, the rest has proven over the years to be supremely right. Many of the current and past leaders in the field came under her influence in their training, and though a few of them have since rebelled against some of her dictates, all of them recall her with awe and affection.

"It was wonderful to work for her!" remembers Linda Lapides, former Assistant Coordinator of Work with Young Adults at Enoch Pratt Free Library in Baltimore, where Margaret Edwards spent her career. "You would do anything for her, because she had goals; she had a philosophy; she could make people understand and inspire and challenge them to meet those goals."[2] Joni Bodart, the leading authority on booktalking, acknowledges, "I am standing on Margaret Edwards' shoulders." She adds, "The thing that's important about her is that she quantified young adult library services—this is your game plan and this is how you do it."[3] Sally Estes, young adult book review editor at *Booklist*, credits a two-week workshop with Edwards with solidifying her commitment to the field. The inspiration she got from that short exposure, she says, "has stayed with me all these years."[4] Deborah Taylor, Head of the Office for Children and Youth at the Pratt Library, summarizes Edwards' influence on the profession as "the idea that we're going to promote books to young people, that we've got to know these books and we have to know our audience to sell. That's so integral to what we do that we never stop to look at the roots of it."[5] Grolier Award winner and past YALSA president Mary K. Chelton perhaps says it best: "Ultimately I think the thing I'm grateful for is that she was strong and she was opinionated, and she was visionary and she cared passionately about kids, and what I got from her was a very strong basis against which to rebel. I always felt that I had been handed a great legacy, even though I've translated it into today's realities."[6]

# The Cotton Farmer's Daughter

Who was this paradoxical paragon of young adult (YA) services and how are she and her ideas reflected in the pages of this her only book? In what ways was she a product of her time and in what ways was she an original thinker?

"She didn't have an ounce of pretense," says Sara Siebert, who succeeded Edwards as Coordinator of Work with Young People at Pratt. That honesty and her self-deprecating humor suffuse the engaging literary biography that opens *The Fair Garden and the Swarm of*

*Beasts.* Edwards traces her provincial origins in west Texas as part of a family of educated cotton farmers, their cultural isolation and religious fundamentalism. Her own innate irreverence peeks through in the delightful anecdote about how she and her sister searched, giggling, for naughty passages in the Bible when it was their turn for the nightly read-aloud session. In an atmosphere of religious fervor sparked by her grandmother, she was raised in such purity and sexual innocence that she later lamented, "It took me ten years to become a normal human being"—an amazing admission by a woman who was distinguished by the open-mindedness of her book selection.

There were books in the house other than the Scriptures—she speaks of sets of Dickens and Sir Walter Scott. Because young Margaret spent her childhood listening to the Bible and other classics being read aloud, "her sense of literature and the cadence of language was much more refined than that of people who were more literary by background," Mary K. Chelton has opined.

But there was a different kind of reading, too, to be borrowed from friends and neighbors, and she describes how she devoured such beloved Victorian trash series as the Five Little Peppers, the Meadow Brook Girls, and Little Prudy. In my opinion, such nonsanctioned reading may have contributed to her adult conviction of the split between "good" books and what she perceived as slight books, an outlook that led her to undervalue the young adult novel in her later years. Another contrast that perhaps sheds some light on her later attitudes is the striking difference between her quiet, isolated childhood where books—a very few books—were the only source of intellectual pleasure, and the chaotic atmosphere that surrounds today's young people with its constant word-bombardment from television, radio, magazines, newspapers, CDs, audiotapes, computer games, videos— and, oh yes, books.

Grown to a young lady, Edwards (then Margaret Alexander) studied at a small college, Trinity, which was run by her church. There she trained to be a Latin and English teacher, and went on to ply her trade at small schools nearby. Five years later, with characteristic spunk she left west Texas behind and went off to New York City, where she earned a master's degree in Latin from Columbia University in 1928 and landed a job in a high school in Towson, Maryland.[7] She was well on her way to becoming an unknown old maid schoolteacher when perhaps the most fortuitous event in her life (and in young adult librarianship) happened: Margaret Alexander the Latin teacher mouthed off to her supervisor and was fired.

As Linda Lapides has written, "In 1932, at the age of thirty, in the depths of the Depression, Alexander began searching for another job.

A notice on the door of the Enoch Pratt Free Library announcing an examination for entry to its training class attracted her attention. She applied."[8] The timing was perfect. Joseph L. Wheeler, the director of Pratt, was staffing a brand new library building and was willing to take a chance on this "hot potato" with the Texas twang. (Although university-affiliated library schools had existed since 1887, when Melvil Dewey founded the Columbia School of Library Economy, most large public library systems at this time had their own training classes for "assistants." Trainees went to work immediately, but were expected to eventually find time and money to acquire a graduate degree.)[9]

After finishing the training course, Alexander was assigned to work under the supervision of Pauline McCauley for three hours a day with Pratt's vestigial YA collection, a few books tucked away, as she writes, "at the rear of the Popular Library in a room where the adult fiction and popular nonfiction were also shelved." Her coworkers, she suspected, felt that her charge was "to keep the teenagers away from the front desk where the adults were served."

## Young Adult Librarianship Begins to Take Shape

Actually, this was not an uncommon motivation for the first efforts at library service to young adults.[10] The terms used in the late twenties in library literature to designate adolescents confirm this uneasiness: "the difficult age," "the borderland age," "intermediates."[11] Nevertheless, pioneers in the field used this prejudice to their advantage to establish YA areas and activities. Jean Roos at Cleveland Public Library set up the first separate YA room in 1926, where soon a poetry group and other clubs were held and a radio show was broadcast.[12] Los Angeles Public Library began YA services a year later, as part of the Adult Education Department, and was holding book fairs by 1934. The Brownsville Branch of Brooklyn Public Library began a young adult department in 1930, and Toronto Public Library set aside the Kipling Room for teens in 1931.[13] Other pioneers were working across the nation, among them Margaret Scoggin and Mabel Williams of the New York Public Library.

In the early twenties, unsuccessful attempts had been made by libraries to reach the many "out-of-school youth" in shops and factories with books to supplement their truncated education,[14] and this concern continued as the Depression deepened.[15] At the same time, an increasing trend for young people to remain in high school was developing, which resulted in a consequent necessity for library service for them.[16]

With the presence of this new clientele in libraries came a dawning recognition of their special needs.

In the beginning the perceived goal was to develop "taste" and lead readers to the classics, the mark of an educated person. Teen's own preferences were deplored as unsuitable and mediocre.[17] This emphasis on motivating "good" reading led in the mid-thirties to the "reading ladders" concept that Alexander endorsed, in which each carefully chosen book is one step upwards toward a broader understanding of the world.[18]

During this period librarians' energies were used mostly to develop collections, to ferret out books from the adult shelves that would interest and improve young people. Some primitive early surveys were reported in the literature, along with articles on suitable books, selection standards, and adolescent psychology.[19] The first book to be publicized as a young adult novel, *Let the Hurricane Roar* by Rose Wilder Lane, appeared in 1933,[20] and by the end of the decade librarians were calling for more realistic teen fiction with familiar settings.[21] The term "young adult" was used occasionally starting in 1937[22] (although it was not in general use until 1958),[23] and the first book to focus on the specialty, *The Public Library and the Adolescent* by E. Leyland (Grafton 1937), was devoted primarily to a cataloging and classification scheme for collections in young adult rooms.[24]

## Edwards Makes an Impact at the Pratt Library

So in 1933 Margaret Alexander was part of a growing movement as she began her work with young people. Her passion for guiding the reading of her young patrons soon emerged. Sara Siebert, who was later her assistant and then her successor, was a Baltimore teenager during this period and remembers Alexander's literary ministrations with mixed emotions. She and her friends would come into town on Saturdays to have lunch and go to the library and a movie. "And she used to drive us crazy. She always had a book in hand that she wanted you to read." Which was not necessarily the book that Siebert wanted to read. "Then she'd be at the return desk and she'd catch us . . . and you hadn't read the book, and she'd ask us questions."[25]

But Siebert also remembers vividly the maturation of her own ideas that resulted from Alexander's guidance. She had joined the new Central Library to borrow, among other titles, *The Motor Girls in the Argonne Forest*, a story with a World War I setting. "Pratt did not stock the Motor Girl series. The children's department referred me to Miss

Alexander whose new collection at the rear of the Popular Library was loaded with thrilling substitutes: *Falcons of France, The Red Knight of Germany, With Lawrence in Arabia, Count Luckner the Sea Devil.* To me war was a romantic dream. Until . . . she handed me *All Quiet on the Western Front,* and Vera Brittain's *Testament of Youth.* I found them tough going. Not because I could not read them. I simply was not ready to face the realities of war. But I had to face her. I had to admit that *All Quiet* was 'depressing,' that Vera Brittain 'hurt' to read. I did not know it then, but my comments probably made the day for Miss A., whose mission was to . . . change viewpoints, to broaden experience and to seek truth."[26]

No effort was too much for the new librarian's devotion to the reading of her many young patrons: "When Alex came along, she was the defender of youth against all these old biddies. She'd go to bat. She'd rush out of her department . . . and go down to the stacks and get something at opposite ends of this huge library. She was simply fantastic," Siebert concludes.[27]

Her reputation began to spread beyond Baltimore. Linda Lapides writes: "In 1935 she received an invitation to serve as Secretary of the Young People's Reading Roundtable of the American Library Association. She planned to accept. But Wheeler and McCauley put the kibosh on it saying she was moving too quickly. Deflated but defiant Alexander requested a clarification of her position. Was she a circulation assistant or a young people's librarian? She let them know that she preferred the latter and that she wished to associate nationally with young adult librarians. In her determined way, Alexander made it clear that if her supervisors did not consider her to be a young people's librarian she would leave Enoch Pratt, borrow money to pursue a professional degree so that she could continue performing her chosen work elsewhere. Wheeler, not willing to lose her, compromised. She could accept the ALA role and enter library school, provided she attend summer classes only."[28]

Four sweltering summers later she had her library degree, her "union card" as she called it, from Columbia. In the meantime she had moved ahead energetically at Pratt. When Joseph Wheeler offered to send her to the ALA Midwinter meeting in Chicago, she parlayed the offer into a trip to New York City to meet with Mabel Williams.[29] In an interview with Mary K. Chelton, published in *VOYA* magazine one year before Alexander's death, she remembered that visit as pivotal: "Though I was unknown and an amateur in the field, she took me under her wing and showed me everything that might help me. As we rode from place to place she discussed ideas and philosophy of the work with me. . . . I talked to branch staffs, visited Margaret Scoggin's branch and learned and learned."[30] By 1940 Alexander had chosen YA book collections, with the help of teen patrons, for every branch of the system, and by 1945 each of those branches had a staff member responsible for work with teenagers.[31]

## The War Years: Edwards Reaches Out

Young adult services was growing in other parts of the country, too: Denver's YA collection numbered 2,500 books by 1941, and in that year New York Public Library established the Nathan Straus Branch for Children and Young People.[32] In 1942 the Young People's Reading Roundtable of ALA issued a directory call to locate all the new young adult librarians.[33] The publication of *Seventeenth Summer* by Maureen Daly the same year foreshadowed a whole genre of literature to come, although it would be twenty-five years before that promise would begin to be fulfilled with the advent of quality fiction written expressly for teens.

During the war years the emphasis in library services to young people underwent a shift. As Natalie Babbitt has said, perhaps with more eloquence than accuracy, "The category *teenager* . . . made its first appearance during the Second World War and was created partly by parents, partly by manufacturers, and partly by Frank Sinatra."[34] The changing status of young adults, as they were needed in the work force during the war and had money to spend, led to the development of the teen subculture, and subsequently, the "junior novel," which reflected it.[35] Libraries responded to this new state of affairs by worrying about "juvenile delinquency" and planning programs to entertain young people and "keep them out of trouble"—films, war heroes as speakers, serious discussions promoting brotherhood and world understanding. It was seen as an obligation of the library to draw young people from varied backgrounds together.[36]

But Margaret Alexander was not distracted from her purity of purpose. Books and reading continued to be the focus of young adult services at Pratt. As Linda Lapides writes, "Simply helping students with school assignments was not enough, especially while enriching titles, those that stir the heart and mind, sat unread on the shelves."[37] Realizing that the young adult librarians were the key to selling the idea of reading, Alexander began a rigorous training program, described in detail in chapter two of *Fair Garden*. With Joseph Wheeler's support, she also began to hold lively and thought-provoking system-wide meetings of all YA staff every month. Reaching out beyond the library walls, she began a gradual infiltration of the schools (which in the early thirties, as she says, had rejected the idea of librarians and other such "broom salesmen" coming into the classroom). And in the summers of 1942, 1943, and 1944 the Baltimore inner city was treated to the spectacle of a jaunty little book wagon with its yellow wheels and oilcloth roof, drawn by a hardworking and much-petted horse, clop-clopping through the streets and alleys with an intrepid Margaret Alexander behind the reins.

And then, at the age of 42, she met her true love. According to Sara Siebert, Alexander had always gotten along well with the opposite sex. "She liked men. Some of them liked her, but others she squashed." Scornful of the stereotype of the timid, man-fearing librarian, "she encouraged us to go out and have a good time. . . . She expected us all to . . . get married—and to be good librarians at the same time." In Dr. Philip Edwards, known as "Doc," she met her match. As charismatic as she, he was a tall, white-haired classics scholar, the head of Baltimore City College—a then well-known boys' public high school. The students adored him, and his charm was legendary. When Margaret Alexander gave a round of booktalks at his school, he wrote her a letter of thanks, and asked to take her out to dinner to show his appreciation. But it would have to be on a Tuesday or Thursday night, he qualified, because the rest of the week he was busy with other ladies.[38] The dynamic and personable ex-Latin teacher from Texas soon won him over. They were married in 1944 and remained inseparable all of their life together. Friends and colleagues remember with delight the affectionate bantering that characterized their relationship.[39]

After her marriage, Margaret Alexander Edwards gave up the book wagon but moved ahead aggressively with her efforts to reach students in the high schools. Prodded by a near-successful attempt in 1943 to lure Edwards away (by the former Assistant Director at Pratt, Harold Hamill, who had become head of Kansas City Public Library), Joseph Wheeler had helped her break through the resistance of the school administration.[40] She added booktalking to the already demanding training of her "Y assistants," and by the fifties Pratt staff were in the high schools fifty days a year, giving 600 booktalks annually. "Ultimately, all classes in the city public schools, grades nine to twelve, received a visit from a Pratt staff member."[41]

To this intensive program she soon added the elaborate and colorful book fairs described in chapter three, as well as several other kinds of programs and discussion groups, but gave them up when it seemed to her that what she defined as the payoff—the number of books that young people were inspired to read—was too low to be worth the expenditure of staff time and energy. A more closely book-oriented project, the Pratt-sponsored teen book review magazine *You're the Critic*, was begun in 1948, and continued successfully into the seventies.[42]

During this time Joseph Wheeler had become fully committed to her support. In 1944, a year before he retired, he gave her an assistant. In 1950 his successor Emerson Greenaway, who, according to Sara Siebert, "did not always agree with Margaret Edwards but admired and respected her as a leader,"[43] carried on Wheeler's policies when he bestowed on her the new title of Coordinator of Work with Young People and at the same time created the position of Head of the Central Library's Young People's Department.[44] Edwards regarded Joseph Wheeler always with great respect and gratitude, as is evident from her graceful tribute in chapter seven of the 1974 edition of *Fair Garden*, as well as the fact that the book is dedicated to him.

## The Fifties: A Period of Fulfillment

Across the nation this was a time of growth in professional resources for young adult librarians. The New York Public Library began their annual "Books for the Teen-Age," and the National Council of Teachers of English instituted their periodic booklists for secondary schools, *Your Reading* and *Books for You*. A volume of inspirational advice, *An Ample Field*, by Amelia Munson, was published by ALA in 1950. Two years earlier, that organization had published *The Public Library Plans for the Teen Age*, a booklet edited by Mabel Williams which included an article by Edwards. Williams' work took stock of developments in the field and reported on a broad range of programs going on in libraries: book discussion and reviewing groups, career programs, hobby clubs, writing groups, music programs, drama clubs, film forums, and programs "to promote better civic and world understanding."

At least one library historian feels that fifties programming was conformist and reflected rigid, middle-class ideals and that libraries of the time did not appear to have been really in touch with adolescent needs, offering only a materials-centered service for young adults who fit the middle-class mold. "Most of the periodical literature of the period paints a nearly blissful picture of hordes of disciplined boys and girls in a 'Teen Age Room' or reading corner, working together, playing chess, listening to the radio, chatting and/or reading."[45] According to Sara Siebert, Edwards' young patrons at the central library were "a good mixture of the young people of Baltimore: black, white, rich, poor. . . ."[46] She gave equal service to the inner-city and black high schools and library branches, and spent much effort in searching for books that would be meaningful to them.[47] This nascent interest in black literature is seen in many book lists of the time. Other teen interests were presumed to be vocational fiction, animal stories, sports stories, popular biography, hobbies, light travel, and war stories and heroes. And in 1945 comics are first mentioned in respectable library literature.[48]

By the end of the war, teenagers, like everybody else, were bewildered about their proper social roles, the acceptable ways for boys and girls to act.[49] The many surveys of YA reading showed, not surprisingly, that teens preferred bestsellers and books related to movies, and that boys chose adventure tales, while girls liked romances.[50] To meet this need a swarm of new writers emerged. For boys there were car stories (the prototype is *Hot Rod* by H. G. Felsen), sports stories (particularly those by John Tunis), and for girls romances by Betty Cavanna, Rosemary Du Jardin, Anne Emory, Mary Stolz, and many lesser authors. ("There is a great need for stories of motorcycles" wrote Edwards.) But other currents were stirring in teen popular culture that pointed to the more turbulent decade to come: The archetypal Bildungsroman *Catcher in the Rye* was published in 1951 to growing acclaim and censorship efforts, and movies like *The Wild One* (1954) and *Rebel Without a Cause* (1955) revealed darker currents in the adolescent psyche.

After her initial foray into national library politics, as secretary of the Young People's Reading Roundtable, Edwards continued to be involved in ALA. She became chair of the Roundtable in 1940, served on a committee to select the annual list of books for young people in 1938, and chaired it in 1948. From 1942 to 1944 she was secretary of the Division of Libraries for Children and Young People, from 1947 to 1949 a member of Council, and when the Young People's Reading Round Table became the Association of Young People's Librarians in 1949 she was elected to the board. She represented ALA on a National Council of Teachers of English task force for the 1960 edition of *Books for You*, was a member of the committee that produced the *Standards for Work with Young Adults in Public Libraries*, and served on the advisory board for *Top of the News*. At the same time she was active in state library politics; in 1949 she was elected vice-president of the Maryland Library Association, and in 1950 president.[51] In 1957 the American Library Association awarded her its highest honor for youth librarians: the Grolier Award, citing her "contagious enthusiasm for books and readings," her successful training of young adult librarians, her "continuing influence on librarians in the promotion of high quality literature for young adults," and "her creative genius and integrity of purpose."[52]

By this time Edwards was constantly in demand as a speaker, and traveled across the country setting teachers and librarians alight with the fire of her convictions. She used her humor and commonsense approach for the same ends in numerous articles for professional journals. "Her office became an international clearinghouse," writes

Lapides. "Visitors from as far away as Denmark and Sweden came to observe her program and emulate it. Letters addressed to her poured into the Pratt Library seeking advice, information, book lists, special bibliographies or her reaction to a paper, proposal, or book in progress."[53]

When she retired in 1962 to her farm in rural Maryland, friends and colleagues presented her with a registered Hereford bull calf—Bullie Sol Estes—to join the others in her herd—Zsa Zsa, Corleone, and Wilbur Mills. The school librarians contributed bales of hay.[54] Every summer the YA librarians of Pratt continued the tradition, begun during Edwards' working days, of a picnic excursion to the farm, where they renewed acquaintance with their mentor and gave skits that parodied and poked fun at YA training and services.[55]

## Changing Times in the Prosperous Sixties

But the larger library world had not seen the last of Margaret Edwards yet. Times were changing radically about the time she left Pratt. After the Russians launched the satellite "Sputnik" in 1957, America suffered a self-esteem crisis and a consequent educational panic. There was new interest in encouraging young people to read the classics and in communicating ethical values through books, a concern which directly benefited schools and libraries.[56] It was a prosperous and optimistic time, and the problems of education and the related problems of the American underclass as manifested in the inner-city ghettos began to seem curable to many Americans if only enough manpower and money were invested. The Office of Economic Opportunity was instituted in 1964 to carry out the War on Poverty, and the federal government passed out aid packages and grants to schools and libraries with a generous hand. "Increased federal funding brought an expansion of services and building programs along with the creation of new positions," declared *Library Trends.*[57]

Young adult librarians began to be highly in demand, not only because of the new programs, but also simply because there were more young adults. "In this new era, it is the young people who are in the majority," wrote Edwards in *Fair Garden* in a passage first published in 1965. She speaks of the invasion of youth, and says "hordes of young people are pouring into our libraries." Sara Siebert remembers, "There was a time when we were so overrun with teenagers that after school the place was like a madhouse." The children conceived when the men came home from World War II, that generation we now call the "baby boomers," were teenagers in the sixties, and their highly visible presence in libraries made service to them top priority in those years.

As federal funds became available, libraries began to reach out to what were then called "culturally and economically disadvantaged youth." The objective was to get 'em into the library by whatever means.[58] In *Fair Garden* Edwards recognizes the changing character of the inner city in 1968: "Instead of college-bound, well-fed, well-mannered young people, we have thousands of adolescents who live in ghettos on relief, without a father and with a mother who never finished the third grade." Undismayed, she remained steadfast in her belief in the saving power of the book: "These boys and girls deprived of a cultural background need the ideas found in books and it is urgent that reading have a place in their lives."

Elsewhere young adult librarians were "questioning traditional approaches to their specialty and reexamining the goals, philosophy, and practice of young adult work."[59] The YA librarian was newly and broadly defined as "an out of school educator who serves the cultural needs of the teenage community outside of and beyond formal classroom instruction."[60] Programming was seen as the key, and "group work" as the way to dramatize the library's services and "break down the barriers that keep young people from wanting to use the library."[61] In 1965 Dick Moses, a former Pratt librarian, reevaluated the purpose of film programs: "Why should we insist that they be used only as bribes to do more reading, as inducements to discussion, or as subterfuges for book talks? Our goal is not only wider reading but wider thinking."[62]

Librarians could afford to experiment in the sixties. With the Library Services and Construction Act funds, for example, Los Angeles Public Library double-staffed its Venice Branch, assigning two librarians to each position, one charged only with finding new creative ways to reach out. With money from Title IIB of the Higher Education Act and OEO funds, libraries began to try out a wild range of options, against the background of the Vietnam War protests, the civil rights struggle, and the Age of Aquarius. In Harlem, the Countee Cullen Branch under Lydia LeFleur held a series of programs in and out of the library that featured film, dance, and poetry reading of original works of black patrons. The Rent-a-Hippie Program of the Oxon Hill Branch of Maryland Public Library had flower children explaining themselves. Don Roberts of the Los Angeles Public Library put on "happenings" such as a library open house rock dance with films, food, and a light show, and an annual Carnival Spectacular that drew 3,000 people.[63] Two of the most ambitious programs were the YA Library Services Project (YAP) of Santa Clara County, run by Regina Minudri, in which "ramshackle, funky" satellite libraries with psychedelic posters and rock music were established anywhere young people congregated, and the High John Project, administered by the University of Maryland Library School, which used clubs, field trips, and hanging out to convert ghetto teen-agers to library use.[64] Baltimore, too, had government-funded commu-nity action programs, which took the form of small library centers in the inner city, and many other projects—the "Go—go with Pratt!" program, for example, which took children and teens on cultural excursions around the city.[65]

But in some places library efforts clung to earlier patterns, and administrators dug in their heels against the new ideas. The excitement in the field was not reflected in the official literature, which still saw programming as solely a technique for stimulating reading. A brochure published by ALA in 1960, "Young Adult Services in the Public Li-brary," mentioned no programming at all except booktalking, and neither did a symposium on YA services, which appeared in *Top of the News* in 1966.

## Margaret Edwards Writes a Book

After her retirement Margaret Edwards remained a steady spokesper-son for books and young people, in spite of the sixties turmoil swirling around her head. Over the years she was visiting professor in library schools at McGill, Brigham Young,[66] Rutgers, Catholic University, and the Universities of Texas and Montana,[67] and she continued to lecture and write extensively. But all this was not enough. She and her friends felt that her philosophy and techniques should be recorded in some more enduring form. And so, with the encouragement of Sara Siebert and Linda Lapides, she decided to select from the many articles she had written those that best summarized events of her long career, her beliefs and methods, and added a "tool shed" of practical advice for working YA librarians. And in 1969 *The Fair Garden and the Swarm of Beasts* was published by Hawthorn Books.

It was a watershed year, a time when the profession had come of age but had not yet articulated itself. What does it mean to be a young adult librarian? What should we do and how should we do it? asked the thousands of new YA professionals trying with no training at all to cope with the excesses of the decade. *The Fair Garden* told them, and it was received in the field like a holy icon. No other book had ever laid out the daily realities of work on the library floor and in the schools; no other book had touched the missionary zeal that was so close to the surface in that idealistic time.

There were few reviews, but then, only *School Library Journal* and *Top of the News* spoke for YA librarians in 1969. Julia Losinski, writing for *SLJ*, said "a welcome change from the usual library literature in format, content, and presentation, this is 'must' reading for administrators and librarians working with teens."[68] The reaction in the field was far more intense. I myself remember vividly, as a new young adult librarian at the Westchester Branch of Los Angeles Public Library in 1970, how challenged I felt by the example of Edwards' devotion to the cause, and with what excitement we put her techniques into practice as best we could.

## Young Adult Literature Begins

In another, perhaps even more significant way, 1969 and the years just before and after were a watershed for young adult librarianship. Edwards's book essentially looked backward over the thirty years of her career and summed up all that had gone before as she searched for adult books that would appeal to teens and sought ways to encourage reading. But in 1967 a literary event took place that was to change the future of the specialty: *The Outsiders*, a novel about teenage gangs by sixteen-year-old Susan Hinton, burst on the scene. The next year saw the publication of *The Pigman* by Paul Zindel and then in 1969 Zindel's *My Darling, My Hamburger,* and also Vera and Bill Cleaver's *Where the Lilies Bloom* and John Donovan's *I'll Get There, It Better Be Worth the Trip.* The next year Barbara Wersba broke taboos with *Run Softly, Go Fast,* and in 1971 the enormous popularity of the anonymous *Go Ask Alice* forced paperback publishers to recognize the power of the new genre.

Librarians and teens took this new literature to their hearts almost immediately. At last there were books that reflected adolescent reality with integrity and literary quality. The Young Adult Services Division of ALA, after some initial resistance to what they still perceived as "junior novels," gradually included YA novels in their annual "Best Books for Young Adults" list, and the sense of a developing body of work was joyously celebrated by librarians at an ALA preconference in 1975 called "Book You!"

Other kinds of books were being taken to adolescent hearts, as the Age of Aquarius rolled on. *The Lord of the Rings* by J. R. R. Tolkien entranced a generation and foreshadowed the current voracious appetite for fantasy. Books like *Stranger in a Strange Land* by Robert Heinlein, *Siddartha* and *Steppenwolf* by Hermann Hesse, and *Tales of Don Juan* by Carlos Castenada were invoked like passwords among the young.

# The Wild and Crazy Seventies

To the background of heavy metal rock and Peter Max posters, library YA programs rivaled the circus: speakers, panels, rap sessions, workshops, exhibitions and contests on comic book art, horror makeup, yoga, sharks, vegetarianism, sex, drugs, Vietnam, astrology, karate, jeans decoration, ESP, filmmaking, video and cable TV production, a watermelon-seed-spitting contest in the parking lot . . . anything that would be likely to bring teens to the library who otherwise would never come there. Librarians reached out to detention homes, prisons, drug centers, homes for unwed mothers, kept files of community contacts and helping agencies for referral, and made this information accessible to teens in colorful directories.

In the effort to reach out, librarians began to pay close attention to the wild, bizarre, and even illegal preferences and enthusiasms of their budding flower children patrons and to involve them directly in materials selection and program planning. As the youth culture became more and more alienated from mainstream America, YA librarians felt themselves a breed apart, and this sense of identity coalesced around "The Young Adult Alternative Newsletter," enthusiastically published by California librarian Carol Starr—who in 1974 led a revolution of "young Turks" to become president of the Young Adult Services Division.

None of these swirling winds of change ruffled Margaret Edwards as she stood steadfastly by her creed in the second edition of *Fair Garden* in 1974. Although she made token acknowledgment of the new YA novels in her book lists, she added to the text only two chapters: a tribute to Joseph Wheeler and a feisty essay taking library schools, ALA, and administrators to task for giving primacy to the information function of the library and failing to dedicate themselves to "enlarging the vision of the masses" through the promotion of reading. The reviews were again sparse but adulatory, and Penny Jeffrey, writing for *Top of the News,* said, "For inspiration, it is suggested that YA librarians read this book at least once a year. It should be required reading for new YA librarians and library administrators."[69]

# The Crowning Years

In her last years Edwards continued almost unabated to give lectures and workshops all over the country. Those who knew her at this time describe her vividly. "She stood straight and slender, with a brisk walk; she spoke clearly and concisely—and had a twinkle in her eye," says

Sally Estes. Linda Lapides speaks affectionately of her beauty: "To me she was such a lovely woman, an incredible woman. I see a picture of her with her mouth open and laughing this wonderful laugh. She wore her hair pulled back on her head; she was never a person to care about possessions or clothes. She had more important things to think about. Not that she didn't look attractive, or always dress suitably—she always did. But she was not materialistic at all."

Even in her sixties and seventies Edwards was an indefatigable workshop leader and still full of contagious enthusiasm for the work. Sally Estes remembers a two-week workshop at the University of Denver in 1963, at which all the participants were housed in the dormitory. "There was a group of us that used to meet in the big, long dorm john at night, sitting on the floor until midnight, just talking books and talking YA work, and Margaret Edwards would be one of them"—on the cold tile floor in her nightie, but kept warm by her love for the subject. At another workshop, this one at the University of Alabama, Joan Atkinson was impressed by the vigorous determination of the 74-year-old Edwards, who announced when met at the airport: "You'll have to carry my suitcase, as I've had an accident on my farm with my wheelbarrow and have three broken ribs. I've had to sleep sitting up for the last two nights."[70]

Mary K. Chelton treasures a memory that illustrates Edwards' power as a booktalker. Hawthorn had sent her on a tour to promote the revised edition of *Fair Garden,* and Chelton proposed to the Bay Area Young Adult Librarians that they had a golden opportunity to have Margaret Edwards speak at their meeting at the publisher's expense. They, however, had weightier matters on their minds. A Vietnam War protest was planned for the very day and outside the very building where Edwards was to speak and many of the librarians were merely annoyed at the idea of sitting inside listening to booktalks when they would rather have been outside chanting and waving banners. "They reluctantly said yes, they'd have her, but several people said they might have to leave to go protest. And she came and spoke and demonstrated her booktalk on *Wuthering Heights,* which was the most incongruous title, given the politics of the times. And I still remember the Texas accent, and everyone sitting there utterly entranced, with all the protest chants going on in the square." Not a single person left, and "she had everybody eating right out of the palm of her hand."

She continued to care right up to her last days. Cathi MacRae, who at that time filled the job that Edwards had invented at the Central Pratt Library, tells of a letter she received from Edwards in 1987 praising her for her efforts to persuade ALA to allow youth participation in the discussions of the Best Books committee. "I salute you!" snapped the 85-year-old guru of YA.[71]

When she died in 1988 her "practical, forthright, often eloquent Will" established a trust "to further the personal reading of young adults." Under the guidance of trustees and former YA colleagues Anna Curry, Sara Siebert, and Ray Fry, her worldly goods were "to be used to experiment with ways of effectively promoting the reading of young adults and of inspiring young adult librarians to realize the importance of reading and to perfect themselves as readers' advisors." Summing up her life work with young adults, she wrote "I am concerned that they read—not only for their personal enjoyment and enrichment but so that they may equip themselves to remake society."[72]

It was a life well lived. In *Fair Garden* she has written that to inspire teenage reading is "the most exciting and rewarding work in the world. . . . We must feel that the job is bigger than we are, that it calls for all the energy, time, thought, and devotion we have, and that it is worth all we give it." "Certainly," she mused, "if I could come back, I would want to be a librarian."

## Notes and References

1. "It is ironic that the award in her name would zero in on a teenage novel. But she would accept the honor gracefully." Comments by Sara Siebert on first draft of manuscript.

2. Telephone interview with Linda Lapides, July 7, 1993. All subsequent quotations are drawn from this interview unless otherwise indicated.

3. Telephone interview with Joni Bodart, July 9, 1993.

4. Telephone interview with Sally Estes, July 23, 1993. All subsequent quotations are drawn from this interview.

5. Telephone interview with Deborah Taylor, July 22, 1993. All subsequent quotations are drawn from this interview unless otherwise indicated.

6. Telephone interview with Mary K. Chelton, July 14, 1993. All subsequent quotations are drawn from this interview unless otherwise indicated.

7. Linda Lapides, "Edwards, Margaret Alexander (1902–1988)," in *Dictionary of Pioneers and Leaders in Library Services to Youth*, ed. Marilyn L. Miller (Littleton, Colo.: Libraries Unlimited), forthcoming.

8. Ibid.

9. Haynes McMullen, "Library Education: A Mini-History," *American Libraries* 17 (June 1986):406–8.

10. "Young Adult Services in the Public Library," ed. Audrey Biel, *Library Trends* 17 (October 1968):115–220.

11. See the listing in *Library Literature, 1921–1932* (Chicago: American Library Association, 1934) under "Young People's Literature," 399.

12. Susan Steinfirst, "Programming for Young Adults," in *Reaching Young People Through Media*, ed. Nancy Pillon (Littleton, Colo.: Libraries Unlimited, 1983), 123–50.

13. Ibid., 123.

14. Katherine P. Jeffery, "Selecting Books for the Young Adult Collection in the Public Library," *Library Trends* 17 (October 1968):166–75.

15. Steinfirst, 123.

16. Margaret Hutchinson, "Fifty Years of Young Adult Reading, 1921–1971," *Top of the News* 30 (November 1973):24–53.

17. Ibid., 25.

18. Ibid., 29.

19. See "Young People's Reading" and "Young People's Work" in *Library Literature, 1933–1935* (New York: Wilson, 1936).

20. Kenneth Donelson and Aileen Pace Nilsen, *Literature for Today's Young Adults,* 2nd ed. (Glenview, Ill.: Scott Foresman, 1985), 551.

21. Hutchinson, 44.

22. See "Young People's Work" in *Library Literature, 1936–1939* (New York: Wilson, 1941).

23. See "Young Adults' Library Services" in *Library Literature, 1958–1960* (New York: Wilson, 1961).

24. *Library Literature, 1936–1939.*

25. Siebert interview.

26. Sara Siebert, unpublished writing, May 22, 1988.

27. Siebert interview.

28. Lapides, *Dictionary,* 5.

29. Ibid.

30. Mary K. Chelton, "Margaret Edwards: An Interview," *Voice of Youth Advocates* 10 (August 1987):112–13.

31. Lapides, *Dictionary,* 6.

32. Steinfirst, 123.

33. See "Young People's Work" in *Library Literature 1940–1942* (New York: Wilson, 1944).

34. Natalie Babbitt, "Between Innocence and Maturity," *Horn Book,* 48 (February 1972):33–37.

35. Hutchinson, 47.

36. Steinfirst, 124–26.

37. Lapides, *Dictionary,* 8.

38. Lapides interview.

39. Chelton interview.

40. Comments by Sara Siebert on first draft of manuscript.

41. Lapides, *Dictionary,* 11.

42. Ibid., 12.

43. Comments by Sara Siebert on first draft of manuscript.

44. Lapides, *Dictionary,* 12.

45. Steinfirst, 126–28.

46. Comments by Sara Siebert on first draft of manuscript.

47. Siebert interview.

48. See "Young People's Work," in *Library Literature 1943–1945* (New York: Wilson, 1944).

49. Hutchinson, 47.

50. Ibid., 49.

51. Lapides, *Dictionary*, 12–13.

52. "Margaret Alexander Edwards Trust: The Lady, The Librarian, and Her Legacy." (brochure) Margaret Alexander Edwards Trust, n.d.

53. Lapides, *Dictionary*, 14.

54. Ibid., 16.

55. Comments by Linda Lapides on first draft of manuscript.

56. Hutchinson, 51.

57. Margaret Myers, "The Job Market for Librarians," *Library Trends* 34 (Spring 1986):645–49.

58. Steinfirst, 130.

59. Miriam Braverman, *Youth, Society and the Public Library* (Chicago: American Library Association, 1979), 97.

60. Emma Cohn, "Programming for the Young Adult in the Public Library," *Library Trends* 17 (October 1968):191.

61. Ibid., 202.

62. Richard Moses, "Just Show the Movies—Never Mind the Books," *ALA Bulletin* 59 (January 1965):60.

63. Steinfirst, 129–30.

64. Ibid., 131.

65. Lapides interview.

66. Comments by Sara Siebert on first draft of manuscript.

67. Joan Atkinson, "Pioneers in Public Library Service to Young Adults," *Top of the News* 43 (Fall 1986):27–44.

68. Julia Losinski, *School Library Journal* 17 (February 1970):51.

69. Penelope Jeffrey, *Top of the News* 31 (January 1975):238–40.

70. Atkinson, 42.

71. Telephone interview with Cathi MacRae, July 22, 1993.

72. Trust brochure.

# Preface

In *The Old Librarian's Almanac*, published in New Haven, Connecticut in 1773, Jared Bean advised his fellow librarians that the library, the Treasure House of Literature, "is no more to be thrown open to the ravages of the unreasoning Mob [the general public, especially young people], than is a Fair Garden to be laid unprotected at the Mercy of a Swarm of Beasts." This is the source of the title both of this book and of one of the essays toward the end.

The swarm of teenage "beasts" were my patrons at the Enoch Pratt Free Library in Baltimore for thirty years. In this book I have attempted to describe that enriching experience and to say what I learned from working with them and the young librarians who inspired them to read. Beauty learned that the Beast was a Prince, as all of us who really know him have realized for some time.

In my attack on the Weeds and Insects (Chapter VI) I may be a voice crying in the wilderness, as many public and school librarians will not agree with me. In fact, if I were not already retired, I might find myself, like John the Baptist, reduced to eating locusts and wild honey. I take consolation from the fact that though he ended up with his head on a platter, he was right just the same.

Sara Siebert, Coordinator of Work with Young Adults at the Enoch Pratt Free Library, and Linda Lapides, her assistant, helped me organize my thirty years' experience into a more coherent form than I could have done alone. Without their advice I might have ridden off in more directions than I have.

MARGARET ALEXANDER EDWARDS

# ⚜ I ⚜

# Roots

According to modern educators, a child should not be taught to read until he shows "reading readiness." My family did not know about this theory, and shortly after I was able to dispense with the dictionary on my chair at meals, they taught me my ABC's. This was done by pointing to letters of the alphabet on the pages of books and newspapers and calling them by name until I could do my own pointing and identifying.

I learned to read by spelling out the testimonials on a calendar advertising Wine of Cardui. My mother liked this calendar, distributed each new year by the local druggist, because the numerals for the days of the month were placed in large squares, leaving sufficient room for records. By consulting the calendar she could tell when a hen would hatch or a cow come fresh, when one of us would have a birthday, or when the Ladies' Missionary Society would meet. Since Wine of Cardui was strictly a woman's medicine and some of the testimonials were a bit intimate, she hung the calendar inside a cupboard door where she could consult the farm records on a moment's notice and yet not make the calendar a part of the decoration of the living room. I was about four years old when I realized that the ABC's I had recently learned were arranged in interesting combinations suggesting words at the top

This chapter was first published under the title "A Little Learnin'" in *ALA Bulletin,* June 1956, 379–86. *Ed.*

of this calendar. My mother was always extremely busy, as she ran a farmhouse without a servant, so any questions I asked had to be answered on the run. I stood in the cupboard with the door ajar and called out words, asking after each, "Mother, what does this spell?" She would call back a quick answer, thinking I was looking over a book or a newspaper. I was well on the way to becoming a fluent reader when some of the words I was spelling out suddenly shocked her to attention. She hurried to the living room to find that I was in the midst of a rousing account of the change that had come over a woman in Iowa after taking one bottle of this magic medication. She immediately took me in hand and bought me some less interesting but more suitable reading matter.

The first book I ever owned was *Peter Rabbit* by Beatrix Potter, and I regret to state that I was puzzled by it. In our back pasture there were a great many cottontail and jackrabbits, but their lives were less complex than those of the rabbits in my book. To me the business of Peter's losing his shoe seemed out of character, and when Mr. McGregor undertook to put a flowerpot over Peter, I was amazed. It took a fast old dog and a lot of yelping to catch a West Texas rabbit, and the man didn't live who could just set an empty geranium pot over one. The sly humor and the artistry of the little book were lost on my practical mind.

Our farm was 250 miles from the noise and "temptations" of a big city. True, there was a small town five miles away, but generally speaking, we were "removed." However, an uncle and aunt and their five children lived only half a mile away on an adjoining farm and we frequently visited back and forth. Aunt Susan, who had nothing else to do but wash, churn, iron, cook, and keep house for her husband and five children, sometimes found time in the afternoons to read to us. I remember dropping in once when she was reading aloud *The Old Curiosity Shop* and how we all laughed when Quilp, the dwarf, stayed just beyond the reach of a vicious dog that was tied up and maddened him with his teasing. But as I look back upon it, I was more susceptible to grief than to flights of imagination or to subtle humor. I would like to say that I sensed style and quality, but alas, I succumbed to tears at the reading of *Whiter than Snow*.[1] All I remember about it is that I was met by my cousins as I came for a visit and was told that they really had a sad one this time—it was all about a girl who was sick and slowly dying. I was given the essential morbid details to bring me up to date and then Aunt Susan read us the last chapter where the girl really did get it. I began by merely shedding tears, advanced to sobs, and went on to howls. I soon became such a social problem that Aunt Susan suggested they all go outside and let me quietly get a hold of myself. They acted on her suggestion, but I felt the need of consolation and followed my hosts around out-of-doors, wailing until in self-defense they created a diversion that made things easier for all of us.

When I learned to read for myself, I did not peruse the best books with avidity, nor did I show indications of innate good taste. I had little access to the best books. In my childhood Childress, Texas, was cattle country in the process of becoming farmland. It had been settled by pioneer stock who refused to be beaten by drought and disaster but instead, by sheer courage and physical exertion, staved off starvation in the bad years and hoped for better times. These sunburned wiry people had neither the leisure nor the money necessary for the pursuit of the arts, nor was reading a habit with most of the people I knew. There was no reading matter whatever in the homes of most of our neighbors and the idea of supporting a public library was unthinkable. My mother and father had both been schoolteachers and our entire family had an understanding of the place of the book in society and had read and enjoyed many good books. Since their emigration to West Texas they had had no funds with which to maintain their family libraries, but they had brought with them complete sets of Dickens and Sir Walter Scott, *Paradise Lost* with Doré illustrations, a set of "complete masterpieces," and various other titles.

Of course, every family had a Bible—the King James version, thank God—and no one made better use of it than my mother and grandmother. Gramp's father, my great-grandfather, was a missionary to the Forty-niners. He packed some food, a little extra clothing, and his Bible in his saddlebags, mounted a mule, and followed the gold rush, exhorting those fanatical men to turn from their pursuit of earthy wealth in order to lay up treasure in heaven.

His daughter, my grandmother, inherited his religious fervor. She was one of the early pioneers to West Texas. In her forties she found herself a widow with six children and four step-children, holding a claim staked on the prairies of West Texas. Living off rabbits and wild turkeys, shipping wild horses, she and her big family fought off starvation and barely pulled through. Yet in her spare time she organized the Presbyterian Church of Childress County in a covered wagon and passed on what she termed "the Word of God" to the cowboys. If an encampment of cowboys had the bad luck to settle down anywhere near her claim, she bestrode a horse and rode out to devil the lives out of them about their immortal souls.

In later years, when she was bringing her grandson Edward home by train from his father's ranch in Oklahoma, she made use of the time to distribute religious tracts to the other passengers. After she had given out most of her "literature," two extra passengers showed up. Whether they had been to the washroom or in another coach I do not know, but their appearance was the signal for Grandmother to spring into action, tracts in hand. This time, to her surprise, she found herself jerked back to a sitting position. Edward had pinned her skirt to the green plush seat. He was very young but some instinct told him that the distribution of tracts, however sound religiously, was socially unacceptable. Gramps' slogan was "In season and out of season—serving the Lord." According to Edward's lights, the train episode was too "out of season."

Gramps lived most of the time with us and between her and my mother my religious training was pretty thorough. Among other things, I was exhorted to read the Bible through from cover to cover at least three times. When I was nine the two ladies decided it would also be a fine idea for me to know by memory nine psalms—one for each birthday. Since I already knew "The Lord Is My Shepherd" and "Make a Joyful Noise unto the Lord," I had only seven to go. In making the selections for me it was agreed that Number 19 was pretty long, but so lovely that we had better throw it in, too. Who could resist:

> The heavens declare the glory of God;
> and the firmament showeth his handiwork.
> Day unto day uttereth speech,
> and night unto night showeth knowledge. . . .
> In them hath he set a tabernacle for the sun,
> which is as a bridegroom coming out of his chamber,
> and rejoiceth as a strong man to run a race. . . .

The old girls were right. It really was lovely. They never fully explained the reference to the bridegroom coming out of his chamber, but I liked the sound of it anyway. I had a lot of trouble when I got to the part about the law of the Lord is perfect, converting the soul; the testimony of the Lord is sure, making wise the simple; the statutes of the Lord are right; not to mention the commandment, the fear, and the judgments of the Lord. Which came first or second or fifth? My mother explained that it was hard for anyone but good, and anything was worth memorizing that ended on the lofty note:

> Let the words of my mouth,
> and the meditations of my heart
> be acceptable in thy sight, O Lord,
> my strength, and my redeemer.

Gramps sometimes had me read the Bible aloud to her, instructing me to be sure and emphasize all words in italics. This ruined the meter because the words were italicized to show origin or a second possible meaning or something else that had nothing to do with emphasis. Since I seldom read her "daily readings" to her, this occasional offbeat accent did not hurt me.

My mother instituted "family reading" in the home. Each night the family must gather and read a chapter together. My father, who could take his Bible or let it alone, did not oppose the idea, nor did he exactly support it. He usually went to bed early and read the Fort Worth *Star Telegram*. We sat in chairs or on footstools about the bed, and when Mother began reading she would gently pull the *Star Telegram* aside, at which Dad would close his eyes and listen passively while my sister and I kicked each other or heard with martyred patience. Then Mother suggested that we take turns reading. She would read one night, then my sister, then I. Dad was not listed as a reader nor was Gramps, who went to bed early and listened with her bedroom door open. When this suggestion went into effect Helen and I spotted every short chapter in the Bible and proclaimed them our favorites. I must also confess that we found all the selections with words of obscene connotation. Somewhere in the Bible there is a character named Peleg, and I think Solomon used shittim wood in the temple, and David or some musician played a sacbut. When we came to these passages, deliberately selected, Dad, Helen, and I would roar with laughter until Mother was forced to censor the Word of God and ban certain chapters from our evening meditations. She could not understand how such irreverence was possible. When her evenings for reading came, she approached her chapter with a reverent tone and attitude that moves me after all these years. She honestly believed that just to hear any part of the Bible read enriched one's spiritual life. I don't know how true that is, but one thing I do know—there are few better ways to train a child's ear to the appreciation of style, rhythm, and cadence than to let him hear the King James version of the Bible read aloud regularly by a person who reads with expression.

Many people cannot distinguish between claptrap and style in writing, for they have never known truly distinguished writing at first hand. For those who wish to acquire an instinctive love of great writing, there is the King James version of the Bible.

Uncle John was the only one of us who actually hungered and thirsted for books. To our wonder, he even sat up late at night and read books. When I was permitted to spend the night in the "city" at their house, I might be awakened two or three times during the night to hear Aunt Daisy call, "Mr. Crawford, you come to bed!" He often read until two or three in the morning, when he would rise, stretch, and go milk the cow which he should have milked at sundown of the previous day. If the book were unusually absorbing, he might read until sunup, which meant the cow was milked twelve hours late. We sympathized with the poor cow, we commiserated with Aunt Daisy, we were outraged, but because Uncle John was so charming, we forgave him, and because he was so "cultivated," we were really quite proud of him.

He ran an insurance business and in dry years many people ran the risk of having their uninsured homes burn down in order to use the money intended for premiums to buy food and cottonseed for another bout with the Texas climate. In one such year Uncle John was low on funds, to put it mildly, and Aunt Daisy had practiced the most rigid economies in order to keep their three children and themselves fed and clothed. This she did cheerfully until the day she came home to discover he had bought from a book agent the complete works of Theodore Roosevelt. She was outraged and confided to us all that after this, when she left home she would have to lock the ass in the storm cellar. She also made it clear to him that she would escort the children downtown and fit them out in new clothes and charge the bill to him. We all thought Aunt Daisy was a wit and none of us could imagine why Uncle John had bought the books. The idea that in hard times a man would buy books was simply incomprehensible. Who was the old Persian who said:

> Had I but one loaf of bread,
> One would I sell,
> And buy white hyacinths
> To feed my soul.[2]

I have said that I had little access to the best books. However, I had access to *books* because Mrs. W. E. Davis lived in Childress. She came there with her clipped accent and fine education and set to work to raise the town's cultural level.

She was a leading spirit in the organization of the Childress Woman's Department Club, which has been the center of the city's cultural life for many years. When I was growing up, she determined that there would be some sort of library for the town. She found an empty room in one of the business houses and got permission to use it for a library. Then she scoured the town for books. Nothing offered her, I am sure, was refused and the selection was truly catholic. Here I found the *Little Prudy* series, *The Little Colonel* series, *The Five Little Peppers* series, *Pollyanna*, and *Anne of Green Gables*—a diet rich in sentimental sweets that did me no harm, furnished me with better recreation than I might otherwise have had, and above all else, did teach me that it was fun to read a book.[3] Since I have become a more discriminating reader, it pains me to think that I never once questioned the sweet stupidity of these books. I was not stirred by them, but as far as I was concerned, they were all right. I never remember showing the least critical ability except with two books. I enjoyed Horatio Alger's *A Boy's Fortune,* but when someone pointed out to me the absurdity of the poor boy's sudden rise to wealth and position, I was able to see that he was a bit too success-ful.[4] The second instance was a clear triumph and the first indication of any intelligence in my approach to reading. Someone gave me a title from the *Meadowbrook Girls* series.[5] I don't remember the heroine's name, but Jan will do. She and her girl friends went for a vacation where they met a fine young man who told them that a most important tennis tournament was to be held in about four weeks and made it seem quite urgent that Jan and her friends enter as contestants for the title, though none of them had ever played a game of tennis. They cleared a court and practiced, and when the tournament opened, there they were. After a series of tense moments Jan got to the finals, where she might have lost out to skillful and experienced opponents had she not hit upon the idea of looking at one spot on the tennis court and then volleying the ball to another. Even I knew that was silly.

But before I got to the *Meadowbrook Girls* I read four Dickens novels. I read them because there was nothing else to read and because, I think, I was showing off. *David Copperfield* fell before my onslaught when I was nine. I was encouraged by my parents who discussed it with me and made me feel brilliant for wading through it. As I remember, I mildly enjoyed it but was more impressed with myself than with the story. I remember the thrill and excitement I got from Andersen's *Ugly Duckling,* which by some mistake was printed in a school reader composed of duller material.

My grandmother subscribed to *The Youth's Companion* for me. I read it with avidity but it left no lasting impression except for the butterflies. I read an ad in the *Companion* depicting the rewards awaiting those who made a career of collecting butterflies and birds' nests. I bought the net advertised and set all my cousins to helping. We filled a back room of the house with a truly amazing collection of old birds' nests and jars full of badly handled butterflies before something must have happened to end my career as a naturalist.

I also read the comics, which we called the funny papers. They lacked the sex and shooting of today's comics, but they were stupid. Hans and Fritz played the most horrible pranks on people and always ended by getting spanked. Mutt and Jeff and Maggie and Jiggs were old friends of mine.[6]

At this point my mother traded a heifer for a set of Mulbach's novels and the complete works of George Eliot.

Since I have become more familiar with good writing I know that Mulbach is unreliable as a writer of history and is not mentioned on standard lists of fiction, but her *Henry VIII* was a terrific experience for me.[7] Brought up as I had been on the shorter catechism by parents who grew up with all the restraints of the nineties, I had never heard people talk of broken marriages or adultery. Henry's unrestrained amours set in the splendor of his court affected me in much the same way that the Pacific did Cortez. As I sat barefooted in the rocking chair on our front porch I wore satin gowns and ate exotic food. I saw Anne Boleyn beheaded and the Flemish Mary scorned, and I was completely spent when the book ended just in time to save Catherine Parr. From that day forward, I have loved history and historical novels.

I loved *Silas Marner* when we read it in school because I had a teacher who brought it to life for me. I then read most of the works of George Eliot but I needed someone to help me understand them. I also loved *Ivanhoe* when we read it in school and vowed to read Scott's complete works, but *The Heart of Midlothian* threw me for a loss and I did not read on. As for Shakespeare, I never knew the plays were powerful dramatic stories.

It was the custom of the English teachers in Childress High School to assign the various roles in Shakespearean plays to different students each day. We sat in our seats and made a kind of game of seeing if we could remain alert enough to read our parts when the time came. If I were Portia and she had nothing to say for two pages, I listened for the lines that would cue me while I laughed at the show-off in the class, and started to read when Portia spoke again. If I had no part, I paid little attention to what was going on. At the end of the play we went back and marked passages for memorization. One passed the exam on a play if he could quote thirty lines, and I always passed.

Imagine my surprise when I went to college and bought a ticket to a dramatic evening of entertainment by Charles Rann Kennedy and his wife, the actress Edith Wynn Mathieson. I remember nothing of the evening but the balcony scene from *Romeo and Juliet*. Miss Mathieson appeared in a flowing, heavenly blue Grecian gown with a golden girdle and began a conversation with Romeo. To my utter amazement, it all turned into lovemaking. This was not one of my male classmates and I sitting at our desks and reading lines, this was passion—these two people were violently in love and I was almost an eavesdropper on their intimate and moving conversation. I had not known that really nice people spoke and acted this way. I had not known that love was like this, and certainly Shakespeare was the last man who, up to now, I should have suspected of portraying it this way. I decided that from that time forth Shakespeare would bear watching.

The college I attended was located in Waxahachie, Texas, and was exactly the college I should have attended, for I was unsure of myself and needed confidence and it was small and friendly. The three years

I spent there were among the happiest of my life and I left the school a well-adjusted, self-confident person, but I do not remember meeting a single person either on the faculty or in the student body who was genuinely well read. I had a French teacher who was sophisticated and world-traveled and knew French literature. My English professor was an old darling who loved poetry, but I never heard him mention a novel or discuss modern writing. I worked as an assistant in the college library, which I thought existed for the sole purpose of helping students with school assignments.

When I left college and became a schoolteacher, I heard my cousins, also teachers, discuss some of the best sellers and I read a book once in a while. I had the good fortune to stumble onto Willa Cather and read almost everything she wrote. I also read my father's copy of *Les Miserables* and a few other titles. Then in my fourth year of teaching I met Eleanor Taylor.

I saw her first at the teachers' institute held in September at the county seat. She was overweight, unbecomingly dressed, and bareheaded; when we ignorant but becomingly gowned teachers from Vernon, Texas, heard that she was assigned to the English faculty, we looked at her critically. Obviously she was a maverick. However, when she walked up to me and made a caustic remark on the principal's address of the morning, I couldn't help laughing, as she was obviously not only intelligent but very witty. She hailed from Rice Institute and had been a newspaper reporter. She knew art and music. She brought with her a sensitive sketch made by one of her friends of a young cellist whose name was Hans Kindler. I never saw such pictures as she had on her walls. She had taken the trouble to bring books along, too. She was dynamite! I decided to room with her, and the dawn of my renaissance came up like thunder.

If Eleanor taught me nothing else she did show me that people could hold points of view quite contrary to mine and still be people of intelligence and character. She enlarged my point of view and began the dissolution of my extreme provincialism. She was also shock-proof. She read books that I had heard spoken of in whispers or with raised eyebrows, and she liked them. When my family and friends read Pearl Buck's *The Good Earth*, they asked, "Is nothing sacred?" Eleanor would read such a book, look me straight in the eye, and say how excellent it was! If a book depicted life truly, she did not throw it down and run like Chicken Little because sex was mentioned or some frontiersman swore. She did not wipe out in a few months the inhibitions I had acquired in twenty-one years, but she planted in my little provincial mind the idea that I could know people in print as I knew them in life. In Texas we ran tick-infested cattle through vats. I thought characters in books had to be similarly divested of sex and sin lest I become contaminated by reading about them.

At the end of two years with her in Vernon, Texas, I went to Columbia University to get a Master's Degree and then took a position teaching Latin at Towson, Maryland. After a few years my career there ended when I was escorting a class down the steps during a fire drill. I had reached the first landing when I thought about the implications of a question asked me by a visiting supervisor as the class and I had left the room. Before considering the matter carefully, I leapt back up the steps, gave the startled supervisor some free and unsolicited advice, and was fired.

Evidently my fall had been observed as closely as that of the sparrow,[8] for a special Providence guided me to Joseph L. Wheeler, then director of the Pratt Library, who was planning to move the library from its inadequate temporary quarters to the new building his vision had made possible. Interviewing me adroitly in his makeshift office, where he sat sweltering in his shirtsleeves, he soon discovered I was a "hot potato." But he played a hunch and allowed me to enroll in the library's training class. Moreover, to his eternal credit he never mentioned my questionable past to my critical supervisor.

Because I was a thirty-year-old woman who had been fired from my "chosen" profession and hired by a miracle, I was determined to make good. As I began working in this new field I fell in love with teenagers, whom I already knew, as well as with books, which I did not know. And so, under Dr. Wheeler's inspired direction, I undertook to do what I could to set up an effective program for library work with young adults at the Enoch Pratt Free Library in the city of Baltimore.

# ✿ II ✿

# The Growing Season

## Laying Out the Garden

When I finished the training class I was assigned, as I had hoped I would be, to work with the collection of teenage books for free reading that was located at the rear of the Popular Library in a room where the adult fiction and popular nonfiction was also shelved. I am sure the library hoped for nothing more than that I would be able to keep the teenagers away from the front desk where the adults were served. I took the assignment much more seriously and considered myself an amateur readers' advisor, attempting to make up in friendliness for what I lacked in book knowledge. To a degree, I succeeded, for a great many teenagers began to make use of the collection. Since many of my patrons were better acquainted with books than I, I realized I would soon lose them if I did not read ahead of them. I was a slow and inexperienced reader but I read with desperate determination. I took armloads of books home, piling them on one side of my chair to read and then stacking them, as finished, on the other. I read in streetcars, on buses, in my dentist's waiting room, and on lunch hours.

After a year or so I began to feel I was doing all right and decided to set up special collections for young adults in the branches. I worked

This section is taken from "A Long Way to Tipperary" in *The Library Reaches Out*, ed. K. M. Coplan and E. Castagna, New York: Oceana, 1965. *Ed.*

three nights a week in each branch for several weeks, assembling collections based on the votes of teenage patrons. When a book was endorsed by three people it was included and the written recommendations were signed and filed in a recipe box for all to read. This took a lot of time and entailed much paper work, but it advertised the collection and stimulated interest among the teenagers. However, if I were doing it again, I would be inclined to delay setting up a collection until I could find a staff member who was enthusiastic about it and wished to be responsible for teenage reading in his branch.

In those days the staffs in the branches were small and usually untrained. The concept of developing readers was not part of their philosophy. Answering reference questions and pointing out the location of books on the shelves were their idea of good service, and at that time I think I went pretty much on instinct rather than on any philosophy of young-adult work. I was incapable of explaining to my older, more conservative colleagues the importance of developing each young reader to his full potential. Yet the branch librarians allowed me to set up the collections and put up with me because I was young and enthusiastic. However, I know most of them thought it would be a lot easier for them to point out the locations of requested titles if every book were in its proper place. Fortunately, because I was so intent on the progress being made with the young people I never realized how much my activities disturbed some of the "ladies" on the branch staffs. I got some intimation of this one night when a hesitant boy came into one of the branch libraries. I engaged him in conversation and undertook to help him find a book he would enjoy. Suddenly I remembered seeing a new copy of Lowell Thomas' *Count Luckner, The Sea Devil* on a special shelf behind the librarian's desk. I hurried over to ask if I might have it for the boy, and she replied, "Oh, no. It's a new book and this is such a rainy night!"

In the meantime a few invitations were coming in for book talks in the schools. I was given my own telephone. Then one staff member in each branch was designated as the "YA" librarian. Work with young adults was gaining stature. These advances forced me to think through what I was attempting to do. I needed to formulate a philosophy, to set up proper goals, and to work with the branch YA assistants to implement these goals.

In my preliminary thinking I realized that work with young adults is as simple as ABC. All there is to it is: (A) a sympathetic understanding of all adolescents; (B) firsthand knowledge of all the books that would interest them; and (C) mastery of the technique of getting these books into the hands of the adolescents. Simple.

# Teenagers (*The* "*Beasts*")

Who are young adults? They are people in their teens for whom there is no adequate nomenclature. For years librarians have searched for a term that would best describe them. "Adolescents" is too biological and should be reserved for occasions when adults speak to adults on a professional level. "Teenagers," beside being a bit undignified, may sound patronizing or scornful and does not seem to include the more mature sixteen- to nineteen-year-olds. "Young People" has been used in many libraries, as has "Youth," but in the minds of the public both terms often mean children rather than people of high-school age and so call for endless clarification. As a result, the Young Adult Services of the American Library Association (ALA) has officially adopted the term "Young Adults" to define its clientele.

What are these young adults like? They are people in their teens who have outgrown the role of children and have become the eager, anxious understudies of adults. They are Angie Morrow of *Seventeenth Summer,* experiencing the poignancy of first love; they are Ken McLaughlin or Jody Baxter, learning through sorrow and pain that one must face up to life no matter what it demands; they are Holden Caulfield, the insecure; Dobie Gillis, the clown; or Cress Delahanty, gradually emerging from chrysalis to butterfly.[1] En masse they look as alike as the clothes they wear. They speak the same jargon and conform to the prevailing styles in dress and conduct, yet each is a distinct individual.

Someone has said that there is no time in life when a greater adjustment must be made than in the transition from childhood to adolescence. Everyone loves a baby. If he cries, adults come running to see what the trouble is. His bright sayings are repeated in his hearing and he may have almost anything he wants. But when he becomes an adolescent he is suddenly expected to get hold of himself. It is disgraceful to cry. No one will stand between him and trouble, for he is expected to meet his problems and solve them on his own. His cuteness suddenly has become impudence and he bores and irritates people who once doted on him.

In the face of all this it is no wonder that he is insecure. But because he is proud, he puts up a good front. On the bus en route to school he makes as much noise as possible, as if to notify all and sundry that he is present and going strong (only adults have enough self-assurance to keep quiet). Boys wear their hair in the style they have learned is most objectionable to adults. Girls go into hysterics over the current musical

---

This section was first published as "It All Started with Prometheus," *California Librarian,* April 1960, 93–96. *Ed.*

sensation. Clowning, funny hats, big badges, impudence, indifference, or even membership in a gang are often little more than manifestations of a feeling of insecurity.

Teenagers, the understudies of adults, wonder what kind of adults they will become and search constantly for patterns. When a model they have selected as perfect turns out to have feet of clay, they discard it and seek a new model until they learn that there is no perfect pattern for personality and that each of them must form his own with this man's wit, that one's charm, another's character and poise, and so on.

For the adolescent there is black and white but little shading of gray. On Monday Poe was a very dull and overrated poet; but that was before the reading of "The Haunted Palace." Now, on Tuesday, he is the greatest poet in the world. One teacher is the fountain of all wisdom; another is a drip, a square, a washout, or whatever the current term for absolute zero may be. To young people, right is right and wrong is wrong, and so they believe there are simple remedies for the complicated ills of society.

The teenager longs to be clever, different, and original, but does not dare break with any of his peers' conventions in dress or speech or manners. He is a bundle of contradictions to himself, his family, and his friends. With all his raucous, objectionable ways, the adolescent is at heart idealistic and would gladly dedicate himself to big causes. He is moved by heroism, self-sacrifice, and devotion to duty.

Only those adults he trusts and believes in know the adolescent as he really is and the rewards of his fine friendship. He is often frank to the point of embarrassment with the parent, teacher, or librarian he truly likes, pointing out to them their mistakes in conduct or dress so they may more nearly measure up to the highest standards. Best of all, he will comment with unreserved candor on books the librarian may have selected for him.

Nothing distresses the young adult more than the sight of an adult attempting to be young again. He does not want his mother and father to romp around with people their own age, and certainly not with the younger set. He wishes his adults to be dignified above everything else, for in his youthful insecurity dignity is the quality he covets most. The soundest approach to the adolescent is to treat him as though he were a reasonable, dignified, mature person. This kind of relationship, coupled with enthusiasm for books on the part of the librarian, will open up the world of ideas to many young adults who may never have become readers otherwise or who would have read on a level below their capacity to understand and enjoy.

There is no age group more important than the young adults, who in a few short years will be guiding the destiny of this nation, deciding among other things whether to drop the bomb or to use atomic energy for man's good. Fortunately they are impressionable, more open to ideas, more ready to listen to suggestions than are adults, and they are more likely to become thoughtful readers.

# The YA Librarians (*Training*)

After the atom was split and Hiroshima was bombed, I read countless articles and books by thoughtful writers calling attention to the dangerous lag between man's knowledge and his emotional and cultural development. They convinced me that the destruction of the earth and the suicide of the human race were distinctly possible unless man became truly civilized. I was sure that the ideas to be found in books would help if the books were read, and I felt that as far as the adolescent was concerned, the library could not play a passive role, that the librarian should do more than just wait on these people and answer their questions. More young people needed to come to the library for voluntary reading and those who came should be introduced to better and better books until they were reading with enjoyment on an ever-widening range of stimulating and inspiring subjects. I realized that clever schemes, friendliness, attractive book lists, and gadgets alone would be ineffective without assistants trained to win the confidence of teenagers and to develop them as readers.

In other words, the training of the assistant has always seemed to me to be the key to selling the idea of reading. None of my assistants knew much about readers' advisory service to young adults. Even the library-school graduates were sadly lacking. They knew how to catalog books and answer reference questions, and some of them were fairly good at evaluating books. But most of them had little conception of the adolescent; they did not know how to talk to young people about books or how to develop a reader. Far too many of them had failed to develop themselves as readers. When they were assigned to work out on the floor of a busy branch, they would become paralyzed by such simple requests as, "Will you get me two good love stories?" or "What have you got that I would like?" So I began an in-service training program that had its repercussions.

Each hapless new assistant was initiated into this program on his first day at the Pratt Library when he came to my office after a general

---

This section is taken from "A Long Way to Tipperary" in *The Library Reaches Out*, ed. K. M. Coplan and E. Castagna, New York: Oceana, 1965. *Ed.*

indoctrination by the personnel office. During our conference I asked him to imagine himself in a situation where as a readers' advisor for young adults he had no problems. In this ideal setup there would be no apathy on the part of his patrons, the book stock would be completely adequate, and the young people would read whatever he suggested. Under such circumstances, what fields of reading would he emphasize? In other words, what do we mean when we say we want young adults to be good readers? When should we feel that a young person is on his way to becoming a superior reader?

Although these questions almost always produced a kind of consternation and often elicited some amazing replies, they did start a train of thought and paved the way for a discussion of goals. After some prodding on my part we usually agreed that our ultimate objective was to interest our readers in books that would help them become citizens of the world. This meant that they should come to understand through their reading that all men are brothers, that "no man is an island," that each is a responsible "piece of the main." We further agreed that our secondary goal was to concern our readers with the implications of citizenship in these United States. This meant introducing books that bring history alive and give the reader pride in his heritage, and books that deal with the problems that beset the nation and the responsibility of the individual citizen.

Subsidiary to these two goals was reading for personal pleasure on hundreds of varied subjects. I hastened to explain that no readers' advisor could lead all his readers to the big goals we hoped to achieve, but that each reader should be developed to his full potential if possible. For the younger, inexperienced reader, the important books were those simple stories that would awaken in him love for reading, especially stories dealing with matters that concerned him in his limited world. Each reader was to be met on his own ground and taken as far along the way as possible, with his cooperation and enjoyment.

It was pointed out to the new assistant, if he did not know it already, that the adolescent is almost always led to an interest in good reading through his emotions rather than his intellect. Stories about a Chinese girl whose love for a man is not returned, a German boy fighting and dying on the Western Front in World War I, a Zulu father keeping a lonely vigil on a mountain top the night his son is executed, are far more effective in promulgating the idea that all men are brothers than sound scientific disquisitions on the same subject.[2] *To Kill a Mockingbird* [Lee, 1960] or *Black Like Me* [Griffin, 1961] might cause a young person to identify with the suffering of others and lead him to abominate racial injustice. The adolescent is more likely to adopt a point of view as his own when he gets inside another's skin and loves, hates, and suffers with the character portrayed. Of course, to promote understanding through books it is essential that the librarian know at firsthand novels, biographies, dramas—any creative writing that will interest the adolescent and increase his understanding.

After the new assistant and I had agreed on these aims, he was asked to check the latest edition of *Books for the Teen Age,* compiled annually by the New York Public Library. Here some two thousand titles, old and new, are listed, about 80 per cent adult and 20 per cent teenage, under subjects of interest to teenagers. Seldom had any new assistant read as many as a hundred of the titles, though many of them were books any well-read person would be expected to know.

At this point we could agree that the assistant would not go far in promoting world citizenship and general enrichment on seventy or so titles, many of which had been assigned reading matter in high school and college and were now dim in memory. To help him become the readers' advisor I assumed he wished to be, I would check the New York Public Library list for titles it was most essential to read and ask the assistant to call my office as soon as he had read any ten of the checked titles so that we could set up a date to discuss them. This procedure would continue until he had read three hundred books from the list. Books he had read before joining our staff would not have to be discussed.

This program was not too popular. To those who had read almost nothing it was suggested that four books a week would be fine and two a week barely acceptable. Some of the assistants were unhappy, to say the least, and some branch librarians thought it was pretty hard to ask innocent young librarians to read a lot of books. Even the administration worried. A few of the new assistants transferred to fields where heavy reading was not required, a few resigned, but surprisingly, a majority stuck it out and eventually were grateful for the training. Some even asked to continue the individual book discussions after they had passed the three-hundred mark. The admiration and respect they inspired in their readers was rewarding ("Have you read *all* the books in the library?"); the staffs they worked with recognized their competence; the ensuing promotions were rewarding. But above all, they could see that the training program made sense. As a rule, all the books the assistant had read circulated constantly, while those he had not read sat on the shelves. The satisfied customers became friends who trustfully expected more and more suggestions. And almost always, to his surprise, the assistant found his own mind enriched by the reading he was doing.

It was my purpose in our discussions of each ten books read to teach the assistant to evaluate books, first for literary merit and then for usefulness in the development of a reader—to show him that many books that would never be classics could afford teenagers a great deal of happiness, enrich their experience, and broaden their points of view. We discussed ways of interesting a reader in a book he was likely to enjoy and titles to suggest as follow-ups if the reader wished to pursue the subject. Honesty and the folly of overselling a book were stressed. Prudery and overzealous censorship were ruled out. Ways of concentrating, reading rapidly, and skimming judiciously were pointed out. Suggestions were made for budgeting time so that it would be possible to combine wide reading with a social life. I suggested to girls who shared an apartment that it might be better to cut short long-winded conversations with each other about the men they had known in their past, instead employing that time to read and so have something to discuss with the men in their present and future.

Although this individual training took a great deal of time, it was more effective than a class for all new assistants would have been since in the conferences each assistant was compelled to do his own thinking and speak for himself. Individual talents were more easily detected and individual weaknesses minimized. Moreover, the rapport between us was better than it would have been in the more formal relation of a teacher standing before a class.

After our conferences ended and the assistant became a member of the "300 club," he became responsible for his reading. Almost invariably he kept going under his own steam, but if his steam pressure died down a bit, the young people with their trustful, confident expectations would start it up again.

# The YA Librarian at Work

There is a theory generally accepted by librarians that people who come to the library know what they want, that if they need help they will ask for it, and that they resent the librarian who approaches them. This simply is not true of most adolescents seeking recreational reading. They do not know what they want. Most of them have a very limited acquaintance indeed with the world of adult books. Many have read a few books that delighted them and have come to the library for a "good book." They do not know enough about the authors of adult books to have any idea who the "good" writers are. They look over the

---

The above section was first published as "Introducing Young People to a Life-Long Pleasure" in *School Library Journal*, January 15, 1958, 218–21. *Ed.*

shelves filled with thousands of books and finally settle on one. If it proves to be a dud, they are discouraged, and if the experience is repeated, they will probably seek other forms of recreation.

When a book proves interesting the reader is likely to go through the entire output of its author, whose collected works may not be nearly as interesting or worthwhile as titles the young-adult librarian could suggest. Moreover, the teenager has latent interests of which he may be unaware. He does not know that he might be tremendously interested in art or sailing or satire, for he does not know about Stone's *Lust for Life* [1937], Heyerdahl's *Kon-Tiki* [1950], or Orwell's *Animal Farm* [1946]. He has no idea of the amazing resources of the world of books for his enjoyment. Certainly the teenager should not be beset by insistent busybodies, but the librarian who knows the art of salesmanship can become a respected, valued guide for the adolescent confused in a maze of unfamiliar books.

How does the young-adult librarian win the confidence of teenagers? By being friendly, by setting people at ease, by going to some trouble to be helpful. I cannot explain this any more than I can tell how someone walks into a room full of strangers and establishes rapport with them, or how a woman intrigues a new man at a cocktail party. I do know that an outgoing librarian who likes people can do it. Before long he convinces teenagers that he has an uncanny knack for selecting "good" books. Many years ago when I was in the most reduced financial circumstances, I went to the basement of a large department store to purchase a dress. A saleslady standing nearby watched me going through the dresses on a rack until she could estimate my taste, looked me over for size, and without a word disappeared to return with a little number that was exactly what I wanted. I bought it and returned when I had to have another dress and could get together $10 or $12. Each time I appeared she was glad to see me and asked about the last dress I had bought. When I told her the type of dress I needed, she recalled the color of my accessories and that I already had one red and one blue dress. She would not allow me to purchase an unbecoming garment and was determined that I would have the best the bargain basement had to offer. She never failed me. If she had told me to buy a bustle, even with my figure, I would have believed that she knew the latest styles, that she had reason to believe I would look well in one, and that if I gave it a try I would be convinced. A young-adult librarian works exactly like my saleslady.

An hour or so before school is out and the students descend on the public library the young-adult librarian should put his house in order, seeing that attractive displays are well stocked with books. He should look over the shelves to check for titles in demand, for unusual titles likely to fill a special need, and for popular missing titles that might be supplied from adult departments. As he scans the YA collection he should look to see what good love stories are in, what sport stories, novels, and biographies of social significance. This saves searching later while an impatient patron waits for the librarian to have an inspiration or is frustrated when a title enthusiastically recommended cannot be found. A quick glance over the shelves in the adult departments will often yield bait for unusual interests, such as a book about the different makes of cars, one on drawing cartoons, or a special cookbook. This is also the time to collect in one place all the volumes of international short stories for Miss Jones's current assignment, so that during the busy hours the librarian will not have to suspend the readers' advisory service to search for them.

In the few minutes remaining before the teenagers storm in, the librarian should repair the damage the day has done to his appearance. He should put out of his mind any worries and pressing problems he may have. No matter if his fellow staff members have been unpleasant, if the impending personnel shortages are critical, if his mother-in-law is coming for a long visit—all these things must be forgotten temporarily so that the librarian can present himself as well groomed, rested, and full of ideas. As the young people enter the room, of course, his interest will shift his weight from seat to feet.

The librarian cannot possibly remember all the books previously recommended to readers, but he can usually recall a title given out in an effort to lure a merry-go-round reader into another interest, or an adult love story given to a girl whose main interest has been teenage romances. To meet such a teenage reader with "How did you like *Mrs. Mike?*" will win the teenager's confidence when he realizes the librarian remembers the title of the book he borrowed and is interested in his reaction to it.[3] If a librarian can carry in his head the special interests of his readers and keep posted on new books coming out in special fields; if he can greet a reader, holding in his hand a long-awaited book, with "I was hoping you would come in today. Look what I have for you," it will warm the hearts of his patrons. The readers' advisor who makes his clientele feel that he especially keeps their interests in mind, is not pretending. He really does just that, letting faces come to mind when he is reading a new book and welcoming any idea that will broaden the reading of his patrons. These are not cheap tricks to win the friendship of teenagers; they are effective weapons to dispel apathy and persuade more people to enrich their lives with books.

There are different types of readers and they must be approached in different ways. There is the thirteen-year-old boy so shy he will run if an aggressive librarian bears down on him. It is a good idea to straighten shelves in his vicinity and to ask casually, "Did you ever read *Hot Rod?*"[4] If the librarian is relaxed and casual, the boy may soon unconsciously reveal his reading tastes. Whenever a title is suggested, watch the eyes of the teenager. A dull glance indicates that not only is the preferred book unappealing, but so are all books on that subject. If a girl who "doesn't like to read" comes in with a friend who is a reader, be sure she sees a popular teenage romance depicting a typical teenager on its cover and ask the friend who reads for her opinion of the book. If the friend comes through with the predictable effusive recommendation, the nonreader is likely to give the book a try.

With new readers it is best not to ask questions and probe for interests. Suggest generally popular titles and watch facial expressions. Instead of "May I help you?" ask "Have you read this book?" Love is the most popular subject with older girls and a book jacket featuring a modern girl is usually better bait for a reluctant reader than one with a lady in a hoopskirt or a rugged pioneer woman. For the shy reader it is a good idea to present three or four books in an interesting manner and suggest that he look them over and put those he does not want on the table. Then walk off and leave the reader to himself. When the librarian is new in a community and the teenagers are reserved, it may be a good idea to be friendly and not mention books on the initial contacts.

After the reading habit is set, after a relationship of mutual confidence has been established, the librarian can begin to consider hurdles. The young girl who has read teenage romances long enough should be introduced to adult love stories. These can be recommended with quick thumbnail sketches that present a girl in love who has a problem. Sometimes it is well to say the books are adult; sometimes it is better to wait until the girl in question has read and liked two or three such titles, and then commend her for her more adult taste. For many girls the next step after romance is biographies of women and girls, which may better be called "true stories" than biographies.

Boys have more interests than girls and do not need to be led carefully from one type of reading to another. With them it is more a question of deepening and maturing an interest and introducing new fields for exploration. After readers take these first few hurdles, the librarian will find that the best readers read on about the same level as the librarian and that some of them can read almost anything the librarian has liked.

If there is one secret to successful floor work, it is the reading of the librarian. Nothing can substitute for it. After a book is read, the librarian can work out a presentation for it and experiment until he is sure that it is effective. In speaking of a book to a prospective reader it is always well to avoid adjectives, particularly "interesting," exciting," and "well-written." Get the story moving with nouns and verbs. Be brief. Do not give away the plot. Be fair to both the book and the reader, i.e., do not overrecommend the book, and no matter how fine the story is, do not press it upon a teenager who may find it dull. Above all, be interesting. For example:

"Thor Heyerdahl believed Polynesia was settled by Peruvians. To prove his theory he persuaded five men to help him build a balsa raft exactly like the Peruvians might have built centuries ago. Then they all settled down on the raft with their supplies, a radio, and a parrot to sail four thousand miles across the Pacific [Heyerdahl, *Kon-Tiki*]."

"An old-guard Communist awaiting execution in prison thinks back over his past, remembering the girl he loved and the others he had betrayed for the sake of the party, trying desperately to reassure himself he had been right [Koestler, *Darkness at Noon*]."

"A white reporter darkened his skin by taking drugs and sitting under a sunlamp. Then he shaved his head and in the guise of a Negro traveled through the Deep South. He found out what it was like to have to ride in the back of buses, to be on a lonely road at night with no place to sleep, and to be unable to get a drink of water when he was in the white section of a town [Griffin, *Black Like Me*]."

A few don'ts:

DON'T play favorites or encourage sentimental attachments. Cordial relationships should be built as far as possible on a mutual pleasure in reading.

DON'T impose an opinion. Let the teenager think his thoughts and feel free to express them. Show him how to refer to the *Book Review Digest* and measure his opinions against the critics rather than lead him to believe the librarian is infallible. This does not mean that with tact and understanding the librarian may not help the teenager clarify his thinking.

DON'T conclude a book is popular because it circulates. One of the most important features of floor work is the discussion of a book with the reader when he returns it. Ask constantly for reactions. The adolescent reader is pleased to be asked for his opinion, and the librarian needs to listen if he wishes to be an effective readers' advisor. In the discussion of a book recently read, the librarian has an opportunity to develop in young people sharper critical faculties and a better basis for enjoyment and to introduce to them new and related fields of reading.

Don't be too anxious to teach young adults to shift for themselves until they have made the acquaintance of many adult authors and have widened their interests. If the teenager continually asks for help in selecting books, the librarian has an opportunity to accelerate his reading and to introduce fields of interest that might never occur to him. Insisting on self-reliance too early is sometimes a way of passing the buck. To ask "Have you looked in the catalog?" in a certain tone can kill the germ of interest in a special book or in a new field of reading.

Don't take books away from young people. If they select books from adult departments, let them have them. Librarians are not policemen. However, the librarian should give the teenager planning to read a frank book a point of view for reading it, calling attention to the book's social implications, its weaknesses and strong points, and explaining what the author meant to imply.

Don't restrict young adults to the YA collection. While we stand behind the books included in young-adult collections, the young-adult librarian is, after all, introducing the adolescent to adult reading in the hope of transferring him to the adult section permanently in the near future, and an increasing use of adult titles makes the eventual transfer of the reader more natural and normal.

Don't think that all this, however difficult it may be, is not the most exciting and rewarding work in the world.

# "The Rulers of the Queen's Navee"
## (*Thoughts on Supervision*)

My husband, who was the principal of a big high school with a very large faculty, once told me that when a teacher came into his office to report what a stupid, lazy class he had and to say with some satisfaction that he had failed 50 per cent of them, that teacher was rated 50 per cent effective, for by his own admission, he had been unable to teach half of his class. While the teacher had probably sized the class up correctly, he had failed to remedy a bad situation. I often thought of what my husband said when someone under my supervision failed to qualify. I knew there was a very good chance that I had failed as a supervisor. This philosophy seemed to me to apply also to a branch librarian I knew. There was always a problem as to whom we would send to work with young adults at her branch. She was a very bright and efficient librarian who usually rated her assistants very low. It was difficult to argue with her as the failings she pointed out in her staff were evident, but all too often librarians on her staff resigned or asked for a transfer. That branch librarian was an excellent diagnostician but a failure at prescribing cures. A good supervisor not only detects weaknesses, but also finds ways to eliminate them.

To do this calls not only for understanding of people and a high degree of intelligence, but also for a lot of moral courage. All of us would like to avoid unpleasant situations. I don't know which is worse, a soggy handkerchief and tears or a flushed face and anger. The very possibility of facing either makes us all too often put off an unpleasant conference that should be held.

It is not fair to let an employee think he is performing well when he is not. No one under our supervision should ever be surprised at a low rating sheet or puzzled that he was not given an expected promotion. The annual rating sheet should be a summary of what has been said all along and no one should ever ask us, "Why wasn't I told?" Whatever might hold someone back from promotion should be discussed and remedied if possible before the employee is passed over. Probably the best way of telling someone the unpleasant facts of life is to convince him that we are sincerely interested in his rising in the profession, that we are impressed by his energy and intelligence, but that we find one or two matters blocking his progress and would like to suggest to him ways of overcoming these obstacles. Or we might say that we have an impression of the employee that is worrying us, and that before a final rating is made, we would like to discuss the matter to find out if the impression is correct. In such a conference the supervisor should make definite suggestions for improvement and persuade the assistant to try them. Whatever happens, the supervisor should never lose his temper or be sharp, and the conference should be completely private.

The young assistant not only needs correction, he also needs encouragement and constant stimulation. We owe it to our staffs to bring each member to the realization of his highest potential. However, on almost every staff there are one or two who have already reached their potential—mediocrity—and cannot go beyond it. These people, often over forty years old, are appealing, kindly, useful individuals who were created unequal. I believe in making life as pleasant as possible for them; I do not believe in calling them in to discuss their inadequacies when the only result would be to make them unhappy. If these people are ambitious and feel they are being passed over, the supervisor should call them in for one conference, where in as kindly a way as possible he gives them to understand that though they are appreciated, they are not likely to be given heavier duties nor will they be pressured to improve their performance. However, if a more exact definition of inadequacies is demanded, it should be given. Whether an employee is mediocre or superior, he should always be clear in his mind as to his rating in the opinion of his supervisor.

How often we supervisors look back with nostalgia to the time when we were rank-and-file librarians, working on the floor with people and books. Those were the days! How often we have secretly prayed, "Oh Lord, let me shuffle off these responsibilities and be free to share the pleasures of reading with patrons. I don't want to be 'the ruler of the Queen's navee.'"[5] But in the end a good supervisor knows that one of life's greatest satisfactions is to see the people working under him wake up and start going places, and all because the quality of his supervision made the difference in them.

So many library-school graduates and others begin their professional careers with the general idea of doing a good enough job to earn a good salary—to give value received for pay received—when if a fire were lit under them, they would become outstanding. In my library-school classes I often have two or three young people who seem to me to have special gifts and abilities of which they themselves are unaware. I sometimes write for the personnel file, "This girl has the ability to speak and write and establish rapport with people. She might become something special in the library world if she comes under the right supervisor." Because truly strong and inspiring supervisors are so scarce, many promising young librarians wither in the bud.

We have said the young assistant needs correction, that he needs encouragement and stimulation. More than that, he needs inspiration. Unless the supervisor is dedicated, he will have difficulty inspiring others to rise to great heights. We must feel that the job is bigger than we are, that it calls for all the energy, time, thought, and devotion we have, and that it is worth all we give it. We need to refresh ourselves ever so often by reading books about people who have felt this way about their work—such books as Jesse Stuart's *The Thread That Runs So True* [1949], Agnes de Mille's *Dance to the Piper* [1952], Kaufman's *Up the Down Staircase* [1964], and Hart's *Act One* [1959]. When someone asked Dr. Spock what he would like to be if he could come back for a second life on earth, he replied, "I would want to return as a young Negro man so I could dedicate myself heart and soul to something."[6] He meant, I think, that the very act of dedication does more than benefit mankind—it redounds to the good of the one dedicated. Like the quality of mercy, it is twice blessed. Certainly, if I could come back, I would want to be a librarian.

When one's work is bigger than he is, he constantly grows by trying to measure up to his vision. And if one is a person of spiritual stature, it is reflected in his relation to those he supervises. Some evidences of this are:

### 1. *He is not a glory hunter.*

Because the supervisor is not thinking of himself, he is not constantly searching for personal recognition but in every way possible passes on glory and credit to people down the line. He does not assign work to underlings and have it published under his name. He is more likely to work behind the scenes and to push the younger assistants out into the spotlight to accept the applause.

### 2. *He does not nourish hurt feelings.*

I once heard a minister say that a sensitive person was a selfish person always feeling his own pulse. In the minds of both supervisor and assistants should be the idea that the work is what is important and that criticism and frank opinions are expressed to further the effectiveness of the work. This frankness should come from both directions—the supervisor and the supervised. The assistant should feel free to speak his mind as long as he has the success of a project at heart. This can mean that if he thinks the supervisor is making a mistake, he will feel free to say so and will expect to be listened to as respectfully as he listens to the supervisor when his mistakes are pointed out. I remember one such lesson one of my assistants gave me. For our high-school book-reviewing pamphlet one of the rules we laid down was that the teenagers could review any adult book they chose as long as it had been purchased by the Pratt Library. Things went along smoothly for years until a student, in good faith, submitted a review of *Studs Lonigan* [Farrell, 1932–35]. I feared parents and teachers would object and suggested that the assistant who sponsored the publication put the matter in the hands of the high-school students who made up the board of the publication. Before she did this she thought over my advice and came to my office to say, "Mrs. Edwards, you are passing the buck to the youngsters." How right she was! I found the courage to accept my responsibility, to abide by our agreement with the teenagers, to publish the review, and to defend the stand to the one upset teacher who called. Each assistant should be so identified with projects on which the staff works and so anxious to keep the ship sailing that he will feel concerned enough to offer helpful criticism when he thinks it is necessary.

### 3. *He is not on the defensive but is honest enough and secure enough to admit a mistake.*

There is a temptation to feel that since we have risen above the ranks, we are pretty good—that we know the answers, that we point the way.

This creates in the staff a feeling of hostility, a glee in proving us wrong, and hosannas when we bite the dust. Utter honesty is disarming. When a mistake is made, it should be freely admitted without too many alibis. Such an attitude will bring assistants to the rescue rather than the attack. No one should be a supervisor who is afraid he will betray a weakness. Few of us were made supervisors because of our many strong points, but rather because despite our weaknesses, hopefully, we have enough strength to keep out of the red.

*4. He makes each member of his staff one of the crew.*

The supervisor should formulate goals and plans for working toward them and should be sure each member of his staff understands and subscribes to them. Then each assistant should be made to feel he is a member of a crew that is sailing the boat to a certain destination. My parents made us children feel that way. If we bought six cows, we all watched to see how profitable they would be. If one died, we all grieved. When the cotton crop failed, we all cut down expenditures. We knew the state of the family finances and trimmed our sails accordingly. When I went off to college, my father gave me a checkbook—not an allowance. He told me what the bank balance was and instructed me to use my own judgment about what I bought. He knew I was a dedicated member of the crew and would think twice before I rocked the boat. The assistant should feel the same way and should be given opportunities to help make decisions rather than be treated as a galley slave who obeys orders and rows when the whip is cracked. If a supervisor heads a big community program, it is a good idea to have at least one meeting annually where the program is examined critically, project by project, and where the staff helps decide what might be dropped, revamped, or replaced, and what might be the nature of the replacements.

In the consideration of controversial titles, especially for young-adult collections, it is excellent training to have each assistant read them before discussing them in a meeting for value, appeal, possible effect on the community, and finally, rejection or purchase. This is one of the best ways I know to teach book selection; no one can ever say he was steam-rollered by his supervisor, for he had a voice in making the decision, and from the experience he may learn how to take a characterful and informed stand with his patrons. However, the supervisor should be the one to handle any ticklish situation where library policy is under attack.

A supervisor should be secure enough to have no hesitation about asking his crew to help solve a problem. Often my group thought a problem through and came up with a better solution than I would ever have found alone. One of my outstanding assistants at the Pratt Library was a Negro girl who was concerned that her ghetto community learn the joy of reading.[7] When a rock 'n roll radio station offered the library time on its program, she cut short her vacation to set up the program. She invited the teenagers of her branch community to participate in a discussion of books on the radio and received all the applications she could use. A few months after she had established the program she came into my office to say she was discouraged. Each week she had taken the disadvantaged youngsters who could not afford carfare to the station in her car. They had read the books she had assigned ahead of time, but because they spoke so incorrectly it took hours to cut a tape suitable for broadcasting. I could not think how she might solve this problem and suggested she present it to the young-adult assistants at the next meeting. When she did, someone came up with the idea that she restrict membership in the discussion group to those who spoke acceptable English. This solved her problem and offered an incentive to the young people of the community to try to speak better English. It was the group, not I, who had the idea, and the fact that they solved the problem made them feel identified with the project. This was not the only time that the assistants helped me decide what should be done.

When each assistant is a member of the crew the more experienced will feel a responsibility for helping to break in the new librarians. If an inexperienced young librarian can be sent to work with a gifted oldtimer, he will often catch fire. Older staff members have often dropped by my office to tell me what they thought was troubling a new person or to rejoice with me that he was so very promising.

Under this heading—making each member of the staff one of the crew—comes the need to allow the crew to try out new ideas whenever possible. Of course, some of the ideas are so far out we need to say no and explain very clearly why we say no. However, we should give the go-ahead sign when we are in doubt, for it is important to encourage initiative. I have been surprised time and again to see a plan work well when I was fairly sure it would never get off the ground. Even a failure can teach the assistant a lot. It is often a good idea to withhold a decision until the suggested project is discussed with the other assistants at their next meeting. Let the one with the idea present it to the group, and by the time it has been inspected for bugs either the original idea will be improved and seem acceptable or its originator will be convinced that it should be dropped and will not feel that a ruthless dictator never gave him a chance. Sharing decision-making welds a group together and accelerates individual development. This is not to say that in important matters affecting the system the supervisor should not take the responsibility for decisions.

*5. He is not afraid to establish standards and expect the staff to live up to them.*

In these days when librarians are so scarce, many supervisors go easy. The administration sometimes worries when people are expected to work very hard. Easier jobs with good pay are available elsewhere. I am thinking especially of the areas of librarianship concerned with the promotion of reading. What does a supervisor do with a new assistant innocent of books? In my thirty years at the Pratt Library almost every assistant who came to me was unread, that is, they had read *Silas Marner, Ivanhoe,* and the books assigned in high school and college, and sometimes about fifty on their own. In my library-school classes I hand out a list of one hundred titles that includes such authors as Pearl Buck, Remarque, Wilder, Baldwin, Aldous Huxley, Steinbeck, Dostoevski, and Hemingway, and ask each student to read five books. This is virgin territory to many of them and they scurry about to get their reading done. It is hard to believe how little they have read.

When such new assistants landed under my supervision at the Pratt Library, it was no soft landing. I always attempted to inspire them to read to improve themselves and for the good of their young patrons. When all else failed I explained to a girl who would not catch fire that in all likelihood she would get married, but on the outside chance that she might not it would be a good idea to insure herself for happy single blessedness. I told her an unmarried career woman with stunning clothes, a new car, and a beautiful apartment is the envy of many an overworked housewife, but the most pitiful woman in the world is the old-maid librarian who lives meagerly in an economy apartment with another librarian in a run-of-the-mill neighborhood. I advised her that if she thought there was the remotest possibility she would not marry a man of means, she should plan to make a very good salary indeed, and that the way to begin was to get a recommendation for a promotion from me, which would be impossible unless she read enough books to qualify as a first-rate young-adult librarian.

Although I killed off a few assistants this way, I think the library, the city, and the assistants benefited in the long run. I came to decide that more can be accomplished with ten experts than with thirty drones. We must remember, too, that the really able new assistants wish to be trained and resent a supervisor who is too easygoing. Those who want to take it easy may not like us, which is a bit of too bad. It is absolutely essential to have the respect of one's staff, and this comes only when one measures up as a person and as an administrator. Everyone wants to be loved, but the supervisor will not be loved until he is first respected. Respect is earned. Love is a gift that cannot be earned but is often the by-product of respect.

I accidentally tuned in on a TV program some time ago and I heard David Lilienthal being interviewed.[8] He said something that sums up in a sentence what I have written about over a number of pages. He said the highest quality of supervision is the ability to release talent. This set me to thinking of Joseph L. Wheeler and what it meant to work under his supervision. He took me on his staff when I was a school-teacher who had been fired for bawling out a supervisor and directed my uncontrolled temper and energy into creative channels. He found Kate Coplan in the preparations department and made her the renowned head of exhibits. He saw in a secretary qualities that he could turn into administrative abilities and schooled her to become the strong head of the branch system. He was so obsessed with the love of reading and with persuading the people of Baltimore to share this love with him that he left no stone unturned. He expected his professional staff to keep Baltimore's reading problems in mind and to think of new ways to enlighten the city. He demanded that every staff member serve every patron graciously—for reading's sake. He was a distinguished captain of the Queen's navee. Working for him meant constant application, grasping things you thought beyond your reach, developing talents you did not know you had. May his tribe increase!

# ❧ III ❧

# Branching Out

## In the Schools

The Baltimore high schools in the thirties were closed to visits from the public library. The superintendent of public instruction had told Dr. Wheeler that he did not intend for broom salesmen or any other outsiders to take up time in the schools. Nevertheless, I determined to attempt a gradual infiltration of the high schools. I cultivated individual teachers and school librarians and found an influential Pratt co-worker to say a good word for me to a supervisor. Despite all this, after ten years I was making only about ten classroom and assembly talks a year. Then out of the blue I was offered a position in a western city where I would be in charge of all young-adult work in both the public-library and the public-school system, under a librarian I knew and at a salary that seemed fabulous in those days.[1]

Since Dr. Wheeler was out of town at the time, I wrote a letter of resignation, thanking him for his many kindnesses. I was disposing of my few belongings when he returned to Baltimore and prevailed on me to remain. He promised to help resolve certain problems and was as good as his word. Among other things, we went to see the assistant superintendent of schools, who agreed to let me visit classes in the

---

This section is taken from "A Long Way to Tipperary," previously published in *The Library Reaches Out*, ed. K. M. Coplan and E. Castagna, New York: Oceana, 1965. *Ed.*

schools and promised that he would write Dr. Wheeler a letter con-
firming our conversation. It was not until several weeks later that I
learned by accident that the letter, when it came, was a listing of what
I could not do and that I was very little better off than before. Since I
had not seen the letter, I pretended I knew nothing about it. Instead I
went to see the principals of the various schools, told them that the
assistant superintendent had agreed I might make talks on books in the
high schools, and made it clear that I was available.

Gradually the invitations began to come in. Having learned about
book talks on a visit to the New York Public Library, I began to prepare
them. Any request for a visit was accepted, no matter what difficulties
stood in the way. One February four high schools I had despaired of
ever working with asked me to talk to all their classes. On the last
Friday afternoon of that month I sank into a streetcar seat, clutching my
modest collection of well-worn book talks with which I had regaled
classes for seventy full periods that month. I was in the high schools for
sure and I was careful to stay there.

No teacher ever asked me for a special book list that I did not
prepare. As for the school librarians, there was nothing too good for
them. I placed reserves on the books they wanted and held them on a
special shelf until they could come in for them on Saturdays. I called
their attention to books and magazine articles of interest and helped
them find defenses when some book was under fire. If they needed
help in compiling or annotating reading lists, I gave it. They, in turn,
were good to me and defended me if any criticism arose in connection
with a school visit. They were my friends and working with them was
a rewarding experience.

When a director of school libraries was appointed, she and I worked
hand in glove. She made out a year's schedule for our visits, which
made it possible for us to plan ahead. She and I wrote articles in
collaboration, attended each other's meetings, and felt we were working toward a common goal. Never in our school visits did I allow the
public library to seem to be in competition with school libraries. We
made it clear that as long as the students read books, it did not matter
where they borrowed them. Pratt librarians always suggested to the
students that they try to borrow the books we discussed from their
school libraries first, and then when the supply was exhausted, they
could try the Pratt Library.

Eventually the "Speakers' Pool" came into existence. It was composed of ten or so YA branch assistants whom I had trained to give
effective book talks. As a rule, we spent a week in each of the city's large
high schools, then covered as many ninth grades in the junior high
schools as time allowed. We spoke in the school library to two classes

each period, and covered every period of the day except the one reserved for lunch. Two of us went together each day, and we attempted to arrange the schedule so that no one gave book talks for more than two days in any given week.

When we visited schools, we took along copies of *Speaking of Books*, which was a listing of over two hundred titles of books on which our collective talks were based. Each student was given a copy of the list. We opened each session by introducing ourselves and explained that Pratt Library registration cards would be available at the end of the period for those who wanted them. Then we discussed the list, pointing out its various headings and offering the audience a chance to "stump the experts." They might call out any title by the number assigned to it to see if we could say what the book was about. Usually, a majority of the students wanted to get in on the game, and in selecting a title about which to ask and listening to our thumbnail sketches, they became aware of the readability of the books listed. It did the cause of reading no harm that we were seldom stumped.

While everyone was still interested in calling out titles on the list, we stopped and presented a well-prepared book talk. This usually consisted of relating a well-chosen incident from a book so skillfully that it would impel the listener to want to read the entire book. Two or three book talks interspersed with thumbnail sketches of about twenty titles filled the period. We often left the last ten minutes for browsing in the library, where we helped the students find copies of the books we had spoken about or made other suggestions.

Though assistants were often terrified before a first school visit, they soon thoroughly enjoyed talking and were unhappy if for any reason they were left off the schedule for one of the schools. We wrote out our talks so as to know them well, but we never read them, and so built up extensive repertoires that grew larger and richer each year. After an hour or so of refreshing our memories at the beginning of the school year, each of the experienced speakers would be prepared to give twenty or more talks. At the beginning of each period as the students came into the room, we learned all we could about them and planned our program as they were seated. A switch in the school schedule never upset us, for if we had planned to speak about a drag race to a class of apathetic shop boys and college-preparatory seniors came in instead, we were able to shift to *War and Peace*.

We never divided the city into sections, assigning each assistant to the community where his branch was located; all of us took the entire city for our province. No one assistant could be as effective giving book talks alone in the high school near his branch as he could be assisted by six other experts who had a repertoire of over twenty talks apiece.

Too, it enriched each assistant to learn to adapt his talks to the accelerated, the retarded, the vocational students, the audiences of all girls or all boys, as well as to average groups.

There is no doubt of the effectiveness of these school visits. Time and again teachers and school librarians have spoken of the wave of reading that followed the visits, and certainly the public library has felt the impact. Also, it is important that young people realize the importance of their public library, its reading resources, and the approachability of its staff. An informed acquaintance with the public library would seem to be an essential element of the education of youth and the Baltimore schools have come to believe this.

# Blueprint for a Book Fair

In the spring of 1951 one of the branch librarians came into my office to say she had invited the seniors of a nearby high school to come to her branch for a visit and that she would like to turn the entire affair over to the young-adult librarians. We agreed to take over as we could not let her down, but after she left my assistant and I looked at each other aghast. We had already given book talks to all the classes of that high school, and there is a limit to the exciting revelations one can make in a little branch to a group of students who have been its patrons for years.

At a meeting with the YA assistants we decided to use the forty dollars the *Library Journal* had given us for a book-week article to set up some unusual displays.[2] When I discussed our plan with Emerson Greenaway, the director, he was not impressed. He was a member of the Rotary Club and knew their youth committee was looking for a project, so he thought it might be a good idea to see if they would back me and go in for something more elaborate. (*N.B.* Service clubs often have funds to invest in a youth project if it is well thought out and convincingly presented to them.)

The end result of my conference with the gentlemen of the Rotary youth committee was eight brightly-colored collapsible fair booths with awning tops, counters, and imitation-silk curtains hanging at the rear. There was also enough money for a large rack to display vocational materials and a small cart, which we decorated with pots of geraniums, labeled "The World on the Move," and filled with books about people in other countries.

There were eighteen YA assistants in the system at that time. They worked in couples to select a theme, decorate a booth, and choose the appropriate books. They all met on the Saturday before the grand opening on Monday, and with the aid of Kate Coplan, head of exhibits, and her staff, spent the day setting the fair up in the basement of the branch. The booths featured such subjects as Careers, Homemaking, College, Fine Arts (art, music, and dance), A Man's World, Humor, Personality (the usual etiquette and personality books plus books of sex information and marriage manuals), Bell Ringers (best sellers of today and yesterday), and Hobbies (displayed along a wall without a booth).

In the meantime we had scurried about to find added attractions for the booths: white rats from the zoo for the Hobby display; finger painting for all with easel and paint supplied; salad served at the homemaking booth by one of the assistants wearing a chef's hat. There was even a ballet dancer to brighten up Fine Arts, though one of the conservative teachers thought the dancer a bit too much. It took us almost a year to learn that these added attractions were subtractions. They called attention from the books and we eventually dispensed with them all. I became convinced from this that librarians should remember in any project to make the book the center of attraction rather than organize projects to entertain people or strain to prove that librarians are "real people." We also eliminated the Hobby booth. We learned the hard way that most busy teenagers are not hunting hobbies and that those who have hobbies have already read all they need to read about them.

From the beginning the fairs were a howling success. After the first year of experimentation we settled down to a regular routine. The fairs were set up in the school libraries. As the seniors entered the room we played a recording of the lively "Gaîté Parisienne," and then they saw the fair with all its light and color and hundreds of plasticleer-jacketed, new-looking books. They stood in the middle of the room while one of the three YA librarians present turned off the music and another addressed them in a style something like this:

"This is the Pratt Library's book fair for seniors. It occurred to us that most of you have no idea of the richness and variety of the books in the public library. In a few months or weeks all of you will do at least one of these five things: you will go to college, go to work, go into the armed forces, get married, or stay home and entertain your rich parents. Now whatever you do for the rest of your life you can find a book at the Pratt Library that will add pleasure and profit to your activity. We are going to take you on a quick tour of the fair to give you some idea of the kinds of books you might expect to find at Pratt. You stand and we walk. After we have completed the guided tour, there will be fifteen minutes at the end of the period for browsing. Each of you may borrow two books for two weeks, if you wish. Select the book you want, write your name, address, and homeroom number on the card in the back of the book, bring it to one of us, and we will exchange it for a card telling you when the book is due. Return the books to the Central Pratt Library or any of its branches. You do not need a borrower's card to take books from the fair."

Then the three librarians became barkers. Each had selected five or six titles from the booth to be introduced. He held each book high for all to see and spoke loudly. Examples of the spiel might be:

"Chapter Seven of this book is entitled 'How Can You Tell When You're in Love?' [Duvall's *Love and the Facts of Life*, 1963]. This big book, *The Occupational Outlook Handbook*, is put out by the United States Government. It devotes a page or so to each of over a hundred vocations, telling what a job is like, what it pays, how many people will be needed in that profession in the next few years, where to write for more information, and often, what part of the country offers the best opportunities in that particular profession. Here on this rack are job descriptions and sample civil service exams put out by the Arco Publishing house."

In other words, the spiel was brief, fast-moving, concrete, and designed to make the listener want to get hold of the book. The barker also pointed out the book lists to be given away at each booth.

When we finished the tour we usually found ourselves standing alone in the middle of the room while the students raced each other to the booths to get a book about which we had spoken. They did not know we had boxes of duplicate copies ready to supply heavy demands. We did a landslide business that lasted until all the seniors in the school had come in, two classes to a period. It was exhausting but it did get across the idea of the resources of the library and prove to almost every one of the students that there were books they wanted very much to read. And it was ten thousand times more effective than sending each graduate a form letter: ". . . hoping you will make use of the public library for the continuance of your life-long education and enjoyment."

It took four janitors working two hours each and two YA librarians working four hours each to assemble the booths and set up the fair. The pressure for time and money in recent years has meant that the plan had to be modified. Instead of the booths there are now two round tables and five rectangular ones—all with folding legs. They are covered with corduroy in shocking pink, bright orange, turquoise, mustard, and teal blue. There are posters on standards at each table to attract attention and advertise the subject displayed. For an exhibition of this type a wooden stick a yard or a yard and a half long can be painted black, nailed on the appropriate poster, and placed in a large jar of sand, or possibly sawdust. The posters may be cardboard in geometric shapes, clever signs, art cutouts, or whatever is creative and good advertising. For example, the Humor poster at present shows a lot of monkeys hopping out of a barrel with the inscription "More Fun Than . . ." The response of the students over a period of time determines whether to eliminate a booth in favor of a more appealing subject or to combine two booths into one.

In the early years of the fairs it was fairly easy to get all the books back, as the students had written the numbers of their respective homerooms on the book card and the homeroom teacher helped collect overdue books. But with the problems that beset the inner-city schools today, teachers find collecting books an added responsibility they are loathe to assume, and the heavy losses make it difficult for the YA department to stay in business. What a pity! This would seem a project made to order for teachers to teach young people civic responsibility. Moreover, these boys and girls deprived of a cultural background need the ideas found in books and it is urgent that reading have a place in their lives.

On those Friday afternoons when we spent four hours setting up the fair we often went home exhausted, wondering why we worked so hard. But Monday morning, when the "Gaîté Parisienne" was playing and the young people were all aglow over the books, we knew why we had done it. Any project that is truly effective may look easy but behind it is a lot of thought and hours of hard work.

# Teenage Book Reviewing

Some years ago the New York Public Library began the publication of a mimeographed sheet called "Back Talk" made up of the frank opinions of teenagers about the books they read. It was intended as an honest reflection of the reading tastes of teenagers to which publishers, teachers, and others might refer.

A few years later we adopted the idea at the Pratt Library and began the publication of *You're the Critic,* a multilithed pamphlet that appears monthly during the school year. We attempted to follow New York's example and discourage any teacher participation in the project. For a few years we barely kept afloat, as it was difficult to get busy teenagers to sit down and write an annotation on a book when they returned it to the library, and they seldom wrote one of their own accord. We hesitated to press them too hard and sometimes thought of abandoning the project. Then we found teachers were encouraging students to review books for the pamphlet, giving extra credits to those whose annotations were published and seeing that their names were listed in the school papers. Interest in *You're the Critic* skyrocketed and students began to vie with each other to have their critical reviews accepted. We discussed the matter and decided there was no reason for us to aim at interesting publishers and other adults in the opinions of teenagers, especially since we were removed from publishing centers. We decided instead to take the gifts the gods provided and allow the teachers to help us when they pleased. The publication became so popular we could not supply the demand with the nineteen hundred copies we could afford to put out each month. From the first, copies were distributed through the school libraries and the Central Pratt Library and its branches.

The board of *You're the Critic* is composed of one representative from each public, private, and parochial high school in the city. Now that it has become an honor instead of a chore to serve on the board, the publication attracts popular student leaders. The head of the young-adult department at the Central Library is responsible for the pamphlet and supervises the young people who edit it. Four are assigned to each edition and one of the four must write the editorial. Some original poetry is included, as well as some announcements and movie reviews. Similar pamphlets are sprouting up in other cities. A display of books set up under the caption "Reviewed in This Month's *You're the Critic*" is always popular.

In setting up such a project it is necessary to have an understanding with the young people as to what the limitations will be. We agreed to accept reviews of any book purchased by the Pratt Library except childrens' books, which were ruled out to prevent sixth and seventh graders from crowding out the teenagers. All necessary explanations are printed in the first issue each fall.

When a protest is made by a parent or teacher, we reply that if we are ever convinced that the young adults are deliberately attempting to give the pamphlet a questionable tone, we shall discontinue its publication, but as long as reviews are submitted in good faith, we shall publish them. Since the teenagers know we will stand firm, they are delighted to feel they may explore the entire field of adult literature if they wish, and they do not abuse our trust.

A book-reviewing publication is good promotion for reading, since the recommendations teenagers make to each other are often more effective than those the librarian makes. Also, although books of all levels of difficulty are included, the teenagers often review books so complex that the librarian would hesitate to suggest them himself for fear of dismaying readers.

# On the Wagon—A Grafted Branch

Some years ago I attended the annual conference of the American Library Association in Milwaukee where I heard Robert Blakely speak. At that time he was the editor of the Des Moines *Register,* and as one of the television commercials would put it, he was "tall, thin as a branding iron, and stood above the crowd." He addressed a general session on the ineffectiveness of librarians in a crucial moment of history, suggesting that we were overly feminine, segregated, timid people who should change our ways and get books into the hands of people, that we should go out into the highways and byways and hasten the day when books would be so available that there would be "wisdom crying in the streets." I was stirred and after a few months wrote an article for the *Library Journal* pointing out the implications of his remarks for YA work.[3] The article had no reverberations, but I fell victim to my own eloquence and began to consider what I might do.

When writing the article I had been thinking of one of the branch-library communities where juvenile delinquency was high and the circulation of books low. Upon consulting with the assistant working with young people at the branch as to the feasibility of operating a book wagon in that community, I met with such enthusiastic encouragement that I decided to make a private investigation to see how one could get hold of a horse and wagon and then lay the matter before those in authority.

True to my library-school training, I approached the matter through a reference tool, i.e., the telephone directory classified section under such headings as Stables, Horses, Mules. This led me to the stockyards where I found an enclosed wagon and a young mare, Sophie, not for rent but for sale—for $275. The difficulty at this point was that the library did not have an extra $275, but before abandoning the project completely it was decided that the branch assistant would find out if there were any stables in the neighborhood, and if there were, the probable cost of stabling a horse.

I was entertaining a last hope that there might be a chance to persuade the librarian that if we bought Sophie, surely she could be sold for the purchase price or maybe at a profit in the fall. That is how I discovered that horses and wagons in this city are for rent. I contacted a man named Stebbin who agreed to rent a pony and a wagon he thought might be repaired to suit at $2.50 per day, which price would cover the cost of feeding and stabling the horse. This seemed a mere pittance when

---

This section was first published as "Adventures with a Book Wagon," in *Illinois Libraries,* April 1944, 132–37. *Ed.*

compared with the $275 outlay for Sophie and had the advantage of affording an easy and inexpensive retreat if the project should fail.

Armed with figures and the most persuasive arguments, I presented my plans to the librarian, the assistant librarian, and the director of circulation. Though all those present, including the chief agitator, had many misgivings, the librarian consented to the experiment. I was given six weeks to put the idea to a test.

A week or so later I went back to make further arrangements with Mr. Stebbin. At this point he had decided to go to Pennsylvania with Happy Joe's Carnival and was sorry to say he could do nothing for us, but suggested we go to see Ernie Frank. Mr. Frank listened sympathetically to our plans. He had a wagon all right but was short on horses. I rather pressed him, as the library knew nothing of Mr. Stebbin's defalcation and I preferred not to go into the matter. Mr. Frank finally agreed to find a horse while I went on vacation and to rent same with wagon for $2.00 per day. I said nothing to him of Mr. Stebbin's price of $2.50.

The day before I left for vacation Mr. Frank brought the wagon to the library to be measured by our carpenter for shelves. It was a handsome, hawker's red vegetable wagon, low-slung with yellow shafts and wheels. Mr. Frank drove up to the rear of the stately Pratt Library building, bringing an amazed staff to the windows when the old gray horse whinnied loudly. (The catalog department said he laughed.)

After my experience with Mr. Stebbin, however, I had little faith that the promised horse would actually be on hand when I returned from vacation three weeks later; but there, standing in a stall in South Baltimore, was Betty, a sleek, pretty mare. In fact, Mr. Frank never once let me down.

The wagon was fitted on either side with red shelves and oilcloth awnings. The end gate was covered with a red board that could be lowered by a chain to serve as a charging desk. A red box with two shelves and a door that could be locked stood at the back of the wagon, so that when opened, all needed tools would be at hand. Supplied with a city directory, stamps and pads, and a telephone book, we stood ready to register new members and circulate books. We had everything but a noise gadget—which we needed to announce the book wagon's approach. For days friends and interested patrons searched the city in vain for a hurdy-gurdy or hand organ. Then our efforts were directed to finding a bell. Someone told me the B. & O. Railroad would probably have bells. I promptly went to Camden Station and looked about for a likely place to begin asking for a bell. After a fruitless search, I approached the information desk and asked half apologetically if they had a bell.

"What did you say, lady?"

"Can you tell me where I might find a bell?" I said.

"Did you say a bell?"

"Yes."

"Why, lady, *I* haven't any bell!" he said in a kind of frantic amazement that led to my hasty retreat and shed some light on why patrons sometimes sound idiotic to the librarian at *her* desk.

The problem was solved at last by the purchase of a xylophone with four notes, which served the purpose admirably but became unbearable if played too long and too near by strong-muscled and enthusiastic younger patrons. The instrument was stolen only twice. It was literally beaten to a pulp. At the end of six weeks its notes were loose and its handle grimy, but the children had had a glorious time with it and it had aroused many a block to come and read. A merciful Providence had saved us from a bell.

As the first day of the project approached, doubt and fear assailed me and faith waned fast. How foolish one could look, I thought, driving down the streets in a little red wagon playing a xylophone and looking expectant, if there should be no customers. Such a small proportion of the community used the branch library, how could anyone think they would read! There was some encouragement in the fact that when I visited the Sunday schools of the neighborhood to announce the project, there had been applause. Mr. Staples, the Episcopal rector who had effectively served this community with faith and works for forty years, told me when I wavered that I must go ahead believing—that this service would be so fine for the young people and that he knew they would like the idea. The Baptist and United Brethren ministers were gracious in allowing me to announce the project ahead of time in their Sunday schools. One minister was cynical and amused at such a silly idea. He suggested that there would be a better chance of success if I sold Good Humor ice cream to cool the people off. I was secretly inclined to admit he might be right.

The day before we were to begin, the book wagon was packed at the Central building with books sent in from all points of the system and from the Central departments. (Only $3.00 was spent for books.) That afternoon a man from the Frank stables brought a horse to take me down to the neighborhood to be ready the next day. As we rode through the main part of town, I felt more self-conscious than I had thought I might at the look of surprise and amusement on the faces of the people who saw the strange-looking vehicle and read the sign: "The Pratt Library's Book Wagon. Borrow Books Here." En route to the stables, Charles, Mr. Frank's driver, when he learned that I intended to drive the horse myself, gallantly showed me the tricks of cutting diagonally across streetcar tracks to avoid catching the wagon wheels in the car tracks. He also demonstrated the uses of the brake. As we drove through the community to be canvassed in the next six weeks, an older boy sitting in front of a store looked us over and guffawed loudly—not a very encouraging omen.

The first ride through the community took place in a late afternoon and evening of July. The branch assistant and I set out, escorted by swarms of little dirty-faced children and older boys—one of whom rode ahead on his bicycle, beating the xylophone. From the first the people of the community were generally enthusiastic, though there were some whose interest was never aroused to the point of borrowing books. When we stopped to wait on a likely customer, others approached, so that we remained sometimes for half an hour at one place. When this happened, the children, who soon learned that the easy books were under the seat, would come from all directions, ask for picture books, and perch on the steps all around, reading while we worked.

From the first day there was never any doubt of the success of the project. It soon became evident that one person could not handle the work alone. Too, Betty would move slyly toward the stables as evening fell. When volunteers were called for, the response from the staff was enthusiastic and many gave up more than one free evening or half-day to help. The boys of the neighborhood were only too ready to help with Betty, and soon the position of horseboy was open only to those who deserved special consideration for helpfulness or who had improved in behavior so much that they deserved a reward.

Because Baltimore people are accustomed to sitting on their famous white steps on summer evenings and because more volunteer help was available in the afternoons and evenings, the book wagon operated from four o'clock in the afternoon until it became too dark to distinguish one title from another. Ten routes were laid out and repeated every two weeks, so that in the six weeks' experiment each patron had the opportunity to borrow books from the book wagon three times. The books were returned to the book wagon if the patron preferred that to going to a branch of the library, until the last visit when the books were loaned with the understanding that they would have to be returned to a branch of the library. The cards were filed by blocks, with the name and address of the patron on each book card. On return visits of the book wagon each block was cleared for books borrowed and due before we proceeded to the next block. As a result, the percentage of books lost was negligible.

During the six weeks that the book wagon was operated, 480 people registered for library membership, of which 456 had no record of previous membership, 293 were young people and adults, and 187 were children. In the four hours the book wagon operated each day, it circulated about the same number of books as the branch did during its eight-hour day. Many children who had "quit" for the summer sent for the cards they had left at the branch. Many paid fines in order to borrow from the book wagon as their neighbors were doing. One Negro boy who owed fifty-four cents was told he would have to make at least a partial payment in order to borrow a book. He disappeared to return a few minutes later with fifty-four pennies taken, alas! from his little sister's bank.

The children dearly loved Betty. They pulled grass for her if there was any within a quarter of a mile. They petted her cautiously and fell into violent arguments over her sex. If there was a second to listen in the press of registration and circulation, we often heard from up front, "I'll betcha a million dollars he's a her." If this failed to silence some doubting Thomas, the children would appear, and leaning between the librarian's face and the charging desk, one would demand, "Miss, ain't it a her?"

The results of the project were provocative; they answered some questions and raised others. As for direct work done with adolescent delinquents, the results were not remarkable, since the young people were working or in the armed forces or married or maybe engaged in delinquency. Only about fifty of those who registered were young people. However, the project was a distinct success as a family affair, where possibly the library can make its most effective contribution to helping solve the problem of juvenile delinquency. The question was raised as to the legitimacy of taking books to people who lived within walking distance of a branch. It was said that these people did not want to read or they would patronize their branch library. These people *did* want to read. They enjoyed the books they borrowed and were steady customers for six weeks, recommending to each other the titles they liked. They expressed great appreciation that we had brought them books and lamented the ending of the project. For each month succeeding the book wagon's activities, the branch showed a rise in circulation, due at least in part to the summer's work. Why these people had not used their branch is something I cannot explain. It was said in some quarters that these people did not deserve to have books. By cold reasoning, maybe they didn't, but libraries are not in business to see that people get their just desserts, but rather to find how they can get more people in all communities to read more books.

Such communities as we worked in were the danger spots in our cities. These people were a prey to every slogan—good or bad. If the government issued a stirring call for defense workers, they responded at once, while many of us reasoned beyond the appeal to a realization that we were already in defense work. If radicals ranted, they made the same unhesitating response. Libraries must teach these people to read and think. This could not be done in a day nor in a six weeks' experiment. Our patrons read more Norris and Grey and less world affairs.[4] They were far more interested in *Gone with the Wind* than in *One World;*[5] but the fact that they read print with interest indicates that in the course of time, with inspired librarians and appropriate books, many of them would read far better books than they did that summer. If they would not come into a branch library for the books but would read them off a book wagon, it behooved the library to drive such a wagon down the streets of its city slums or to adopt some better means of influencing people to read and think.

A horse and wagon was certainly not the only solution to the libraries' problem; it was probably not even one of the best solutions, but our success seemed so closely connected with certain elements peculiar to our project that it might be of some profit to attempt to isolate and define these elements. In the first place, the slow motion of the equipage allowed time for many more personal contacts than would have been possible with a faster and better equipped gasoline-propelled bookmobile. The novelty of the project attracted attention, which made subsequent contacts easy. The friendly simplicity of the entire outfit made it quite easy to do away completely with institutional formality and afforded the librarian an excellent opportunity to "visit" with her neighbors and newly acquired friends.

Too often a wide gulf lay between our librarians and the people they wished to serve. In these poorer districts where tough-fibered men did hard physical labor and the women were too often the ill-nourished slaves of large families, our college-bred career girls housed in institutional buildings and representing "culture" had very little appeal for their possible clientele. There just was not enough in common between them. It was much simpler for a sunburned librarian driving a horse to quickly establish a bond of interest with the woman and her family seated on their doorstep.

While such a project seemed fruitful for the community, it was of inestimable value to the librarians. Those who worked on the wagon could understand why a Negro woman who lived with her eight children in a three-room apartment up a swaying stairway had not had time to broaden her cultural interests; why in such a family the older children returned the books. There just wasn't anywhere to put the book where the baby could not find it. The librarian could soon see why Mrs. Norris' *Angel in the House* [1933] was a fine book for this woman. Many matters that were merely irritating in the library became little human tragedies when seen against their backgrounds. These people had fine things to give us, too. They taught us much about courage and humor, strength and patience.

Mrs. Darden, a Negro who lived in a noisy run-down district, was anxious to have her five daughters read and love books. She herself had had books "when I lived in Virginia." She registered and sent for a book on United States history and had each of her girls take cards. When the book wagon drew up to her street, her five daughters appeared wearing freshly ironed dresses in celebration of the wagon's appearance and they all took books.

The white women who lived on the cobblestone alley where the stables were located loved the evening air, which seemed stale to us. They bathed their babies and made an occasion of sitting out until bedtime. The men at the stables were as gallant as the men who preside over cotillions. They had a rich sense of humor, too. One afternoon a man selling watermelons stopped us to say, "Hey! Why don't you buy a watermelon?" We replied, "Why don't you borrow a book?" He said, "If I borrow a book, will you buy a melon?" We traded and parted with amusement on all sides of the street.

One night I stabled the horse long after dark and started up the cobblestone alley towards the bus stop when I heard bare feet padding behind me and a woman calling, "Hey, Miss!" I turned to face the woman, who lived near the stable. "Say," she said, "have you got any books about being a woman?" I told her I would bring her one the next day. I brought her Zabriski's *Mother and Baby Care in Pictures* [1941], with which she was perfectly delighted, and she asked for more books like it. I brought her another dealing with "the facts of life," which she did not like. I brought still another, which she did not care for either. Then I asked her why she liked the first book but not the other two, saying she would have to give me some help in making the selections. "Well, you see, Miss," she said, "I can't read."

We librarians need to learn anew that people are the same everywhere. We are too inclined to go out to bless these people when we try to help them. We forget that we are often victims of a kind of precious insularity and that these people with fewer opportunities but more hardiness can often send us home with a greater blessing than we gave them.

The second summer I left this district for a crowded, all-Negro slum across town that was being given special attention by the Department of Public Welfare. In my first summer I had been dismayed by the number of white women who sat on their steps in the hot afternoons, preferring to stare out at their sordid surroundings rather than to read any book ever published. The men beat their children unmercifully. One woman whose son had stolen my purse begged me not to tell his father, as she could not stand to see the beating he would give the boy. With both men and women, interest was almost entirely in the physical.

I drove into the Negro slum the first afternoon, wondering what it would be like and fearful again of what my reception might be, when an old woman leaned out of a second-floor window and called down, "Do you have any poetry books?" When I said I had, she asked, "Have you got one with Rabbi Ben Ezra?" What a wonderful omen! From the beginning I met with warm friendliness and a far more heartening interest in books than I had encountered the first summer. There was a ready response to poetry and music. Young and old borrowed song books. Adults borrowed Bibles, religious books of many kinds, and collections of spirituals. There was an unexpected demand from adults for textbooks—geographies, histories, spellers, arithmetics "like we used to have in school." Two men wanted books on "how to talk right." One huckster left his wagon to ask for a book on the multiplication tables. Dictionaries and books by and about Negroes were requested. Evidently the motion pictures had influenced the demand for fiction, as better than half the novels borrowed were by authors whose books had recently been made into movies. The housewives were especially interested in cookbooks, and on my limited budget I could not begin to supply the demand. One afternoon I drove down an alley where some elderly women were sitting on their front steps. I asked them if they would like to look over the books on the wagon and one of the old women said, "I don't want any book in the world unless it tells me how to make watermelon pickles." Before I had started the season, I had gone to the gas and electric company for any giveaway materials they might have. I looked in one of their pamphlets and there by God's grace was a recipe for watermelon pickles. Amid general rejoicing I distributed pamphlets to all the old ladies to keep.

From four o'clock in the afternoon until dark the little red wagon moved up and down the streets. Since the horse was still stabled at Cross Street, when business was over for the day a lighted lantern was hung under the wagon and the trip across town was made.

The librarians who worked with the wagon were treated with the greatest kindness and help for any emergency was always at hand. My horse that second summer was named Berry for "liberry," and the afternoon he fell down on Gay Street was a tense moment. I was terrified that he might have broken a leg, and that if I forced him to get up, the leg just might be hanging by a tendon. However, several people recruited from the sidewalks and saloons by helpful onlookers got the horse up, straw hat and all, to reveal that he was in good condition and that his reluctance to get up was probably nothing more than boredom with a project others found more interesting.

In the thirty-eight days of that summer, 725 new members were registered, of whom about half were adults, and over four thousand books were circulated.

Librarians wonder why people living in a community with a branch library do not make better use of it. I could see by visiting with the women of this neighborhood why they were not members of the library. Many of them worked in a suburban household all day, returning at night exhausted to an unkempt house, children who were demanding attention, and a hungry, impatient husband. There simply was no time to make oneself presentable and walk even a few blocks to select a book, especially if one did not know what book one wanted and was timid about going into an institution that seemed a bit formidable. The men did not even know they wanted a book until they saw helpful titles readily available.

I worked the next summer in the same district, but after that, marriage ended the project. I was forty-two when a distinguished gentleman asked me to marry him. I had resigned myself to single blessedness and this was too much. It took about eighteen hours a day to keep the wagon rolling, and I was so in love. No other librarian could drive a horse or stand up physically to the work, so it all ended.

I should like to say in conclusion that I doubt if libraries will ever get books into the hands of the masses of the inner city until they get out of their institutions and onto the streets. I am not suggesting the book wagon as the only answer, but I am saying that librarians who know books and like people must go up and down the streets of slums selling the idea of reading and persuading people to reach out for books. We know from a century of experience that only a very few will take the initiative and come to us.

# ❧ IV ❧

# Thinning the Plants

When the YA librarian considers undertaking a new activity, he should think over the activities in which he is already engaged to see if there is room for a new one or if the new idea seems promising enough to justify dropping an established project. Because I was inexperienced and sold on my job, I had to learn the hard way that there are only twenty-four hours in each day, that human beings have limitations, and that it is better to be effective than all-inclusive. I learned these things from three projects.

## A Book Club

About the time I was setting up the YA collections in the branches, one of the younger trained librarians asked me if I would like to form a reading club at her branch and I jumped at the chance. Her community was roughly half Italian and half Jewish. From the gay Italians we recruited one brilliant girl.[1] The other members were the children of Jewish immigrants freshly arrived from Europe with scarves on their heads, large families, and little money, but with character and minds enriched by their Continental background.

---

This section is taken from "A Long Way to Tipperary," published in *The Library Reaches Out*, ed. K. M. Coplan and E. Castagna, New York: Oceana, 1965. *Ed.*

The librarian suggested we spend ten dollars monthly from her book budget to purchase books we thought would enrich the branch collection. To do this the club members and I read five or six books before each meeting, discussed them, compared them, argued, read reviews, and then took a vote to decide which to add to our collection.

As a book club it was a great success, but it just about finished me. I had to read every book, collect professional reviews, plan the reading for the next meeting, send extra copies of all the books to the branch for club members to read, and then lead the discussions. I took counsel with myself after a year and came to the conclusion that something had to give. Because I had to read all the books considered for purchase in order to make the discussions meaningful, I was falling behind in my reading for my patrons at the central library, as well as for those I worked with three nights a week in the branches. My book background was too weak to stand the strain and my good readers were outdistancing me. While the club was stimulating and obviously meant a great deal to the members, I wondered if it was fair to spend an evening with those few superior youngsters and leave fifty or so unattended at a branch. I was at that time the one readers' advisor for young adults in the system and there was no one to take my place when I was away.

There is the old story of Moody and Sankey that tells how the older of the evangelists, I think it was Moody, preached one night to an audience of one young man, but the youth turned out to be Sankey.[2] Maybe among the little group in the meeting room will sit the future Governor of the state. On the other hand, he just might be in the group wandering unassisted on the floor of the library. We have no way of telling, but the odds are in favor of his being in the larger group.

Many inexperienced young assistants wished to organize a book club but I often discouraged them. Certainly if large enough groups attend the meeting regularly, there is an argument in their favor; but most clubs are foredoomed to failure because teenagers do not read the books assigned for discussion. They are honestly too busy with schoolwork, homework, TV, sports, jobs, and dances to read for discussion and they usually drop out. Nor should YA librarians set up clubs that are not concerned with books, films, or library materials. Activities that keep youngsters off the streets, that give them games to play and entertain them, are the province of social workers.

I may be rationalizing here. While clubs seem unprofitable to me in comparison with other activities, another librarian might find them the best way to reach the young adults of a community. Each YA librarian decides for himself on what projects to spend time and energy in order to bring the most books to the most young people.

# The UNY and I

When the United Nations Youth (UNY) was organized in Baltimore, I was persuaded to be its first sponsor. It seemed to me a good way to establish rapport with a large group of intelligent teenagers from most of the Baltimore high schools and at the same time to promote interest in world problems which, hopefully, might lead to reading. This seemed too good to pass up, and I went into action.

We prepared a float for a Navy Day parade; we attended a Chinese dinner where we ate chop suey with chop sticks and listened to Chinese speakers; we sent delegates as observers to Lake Success, to a Security Council meeting, and to other places. When they returned, they spoke to service clubs, school assemblies, and civic groups. We sent a large delegation to the New York *Herald Tribune*'s annual youth forum featuring students from South America and brought the visiting students back to Baltimore for a memorable weekend.

With all this, many of the UNY became better citizens of the world, but as I looked back over that year, I found it difficult to balance accounts. Under profits could be listed the breadth of vision and increased sense of responsibility for the state of the world that was fostered in many young people. On the other hand, I remembered the many Sunday afternoons when it was more urgent to attend a meeting of the UNY than to play tennis with a long-suffering husband. I remembered the endless telephoning and bookkeeping and extra quarters found among the papers on my desk at the library. There were the times when the youngsters did not show up as they had promised and I sealed and addressed important notices to get them out on time. But worst of all were the afternoons when crises arose, i.e., when the chop suey simply had to be sent to the changed meeting place by five o'clock or else. As I dialed numbers frantically on the telephone on my library desk, some youngster invariably edged up to ask, "Would you get me a book about an eccentric person?" Though never said aloud, my smothered answer to such a question was "I'll wring your neck!" How low can a librarian sink?

Some years ago two books were published at the same time. In one, *The Importance of Living* [1937], Lin Yutang said that the trouble with our Western world was its bustle and hurry. He described an old Chinese philosopher clothed in a white silk robe who stood for hours with an exquisite fan in hand contemplating a flower. In the other book, *Madame Curie* [Eve Curie, 1937], the discoverer of radium told how day

---

This section was published as "The Librarian and the United Nations Youth," in *Top of the News*, September 1948, 14–17. *Ed.*

after day she stirred a boiling cauldron with a stick almost as big as herself. "It was killing work," she said.

Now what is one to do? Contemplate a flower or be a ball of fire? And if one is too big a ball of fire, who is going to do the library work?

# The Book Week Parties

For two years we celebrated Book Week with a teenage party. In the early forties when *Seventeenth Summer* [Daly, 1942] revolutionized teenage reading, we invited all the high-school students to a masquerade party at the central library, with Maureen Daly and the editor of *Seventeen* magazine as speakers. The guests were to come disguised as characters in books. There was apprehension in some quarters, as this was to be an integrated party and in Baltimore at that time such a thing was almost unheard of. The affair was quite successful but it was the ninth and tenth graders rather than the juniors and seniors who came in the largest numbers. For Southern High School it was truly a gala affair. An understanding high-school librarian helped the students with their costumes, which took most of the prizes and gave the students courage to make their first trip across Baltimore Street into the heart of the big city. The autographed copies of *Seventeenth Summer* were the first books most of them had ever owned. One of the Baltimore *Sun*'s best photographers took pictures of the most attractive costumes for the photogravure section on the Sunday paper. It was a big night.

The next year's Book Week party featured the sportswriter and author John Tunis. The day of the event was a rainy Sunday afternoon. There was a fair crowd, the boys loved Mr. Tunis, and the guests had a good time, but it seemed to me these parties were too difficult to plan for, too time-consuming, and too unrelated to reading. Here again, an evaluation of our program seemed in order. In making decisions about which projects to eliminate and which to keep, there are always intangibles to consider. One never can measure the extent to which readers have been inspired or enriched. However, circulation figures give us a pretty good indication of the effectiveness of a library activity. Although our guests enjoyed our parties and they were good public relations, they did not influence young people to read books as had some of our other activities, so we eliminated the Book Week parties.

# ❧ V ❧

# Provender for the "Beasts"

## What Is the Best Food for the "Beasts"?
## Classics? "Pleasant" Books? Realism?

Years ago in a Texas town a doctor I knew was returning from a sick call late at night when he heard the sound of running feet. Soon a young man came tearing past him, only to be outdistanced by a black cat that streaked across his path. "Son of a gun!" the outraged boy shouted. "Son of a gun!"

For years adults concerned with the reading of teenagers have been racing another kind of black cat—this one not so much a symbol of bad luck as of personal corruption. These adults cherish certain beliefs about what teenagers should or should not read. When these beliefs are violated, they are outraged. What escapes them is that these precepts, while seemly, are not always sound.

Let's look at a few of these precepts.

*Give him a classic!* Any literate person is heartily in favor of the classics, but because a book is a classic it does not as a matter of course become a rich reading experience for everyone. In fact, the depth of philosophy, the subtle probing of complex human motives in the great

---

The first part of this section was originally published as "A Time When It's Best to Read and Let Read," *New York Times Book Review,* May 8, 1960. *Ed.*

books, often dismay the inexperienced reader. The teenager who has never known consuming passion cannot understand how Anna Karenina could desert a good husband and a sweet child for another man. Many teenagers like *A Tale of Two Cities* but are bored by Dickens' leisurely progress through the adventures of *Dombey and Son* and *Martin Chuzzlewit*. With the exception of *Ivanhoe* and some of the Waverly novels, Scott has little interest for today's teenagers. This is not to say that young people do not like classics. They adore *Jane Eyre, Pride and Prejudice, Wuthering Heights,* and others they can understand.

Is it possible that some librarians insist on the classics in order to play safe, to avoid reading widely and forming opinions on modern writing, and to escape criticism when recommending to teenagers books to which their parents might object? For example, if Shakespeare writes a sonnet to a beautiful boy, we pass over it lightly because the master is above censure, but if Mary Renault touches on the same subject in *The King Must Die* [1958], we hope no parent will protest its inclusion on a high-school list. Marriage without benefit of clergy is one thing for Hester Prynne but something else for little Teale Eye in Guthrie's *The Big Sky* [1947].

We must make the best writing of all time available to teenagers. We should offer them the classics they can understand and then seek out the best of modern writing, defending it when necessary.

*Keep it pleasant!* Though the floods descend, some well-meaning adults would intone this old chant:

> It is not raining rain to me,
> It's raining violets.

We do not want our adolescents to see the seamy side of life. We do not want them to suffer pain and unhappiness, and if we could, we would prolong the age of innocence indefinitely. Of course, if we should succeed in our efforts to do this, we would at the same time rob our young people of the opportunity to build strength of character and incapacitate them for the crises they are sure to meet.

Hunger and pain are the lot of millions of people; war has ravaged the earth periodically; love is not always constant; and death will end us all. But *mirabile dictu*, the spirit of man can rise above every disaster. Young people are not devastated by reading about unpleasantness. (Even as children, they applauded as the little pig boiled the big, bad wolf alive for supper.) We must let teenagers read of life as it is and learn how people of courage get the best of it. *A Tree Grows in Brooklyn, The Good Earth, Hiroshima, All Quiet on the Western Front, Manchild in the*

*Promised Land,* and other books that present life truly are part of the heritage of the adolescent.[1]

*One good book can work a miracle.* Americans are people of faith. We believe the product recommended on TV is as superior as the commercial announcer says it is. If a writer on health is enthusiastic about blackstrap molasses, we eat it until another recommends honey. We have been told and do believe that one "good" book can work a miracle while one "bad" one can guide the reader down the wrong path.

There are no reliable studies on the effects of reading. However, psychiatrists tell us that if children are given enough love and a sense of security by their parents, it is very difficult indeed to upset their emotional balance. Children who do not gain this sense of security are likely to be upset eventually by the first bottle of beer they drink, the first encounter they have with sex, the first "bad" book they read.

We want teenagers to read the best books for we feel sure that one's accumulated reading has a decided effect. But if one or two "bad" books find their way into the adolescent's hands, it is likely their effect will be neutralized if many good books are also read.

*Facts are better than fiction.* Certainly we get essential information from factual books, but it is experience we need most. If we would live richly, we can expand our lives more by sailing down the Nile with Cleopatra, looking at the cherry trees with Housman, or sweating it out to triumph at long last with Moss Hart than we can by gathering all available information on Egypt, raising cherries, or writing for the theatre.

*Sex isn't necessary.* Many adults seem to think that if sex is not mentioned to adolescents, it will go away. On the contrary, it is here to stay and teenagers are avidly interested in it. They will find out all they can about it and wise adults will make available reliable books that tell them what they wish to know. There are excellent factual books on the market, but the best novels on the subject go beyond the facts to the emotional implications of love. *Of Human Bondage, Wuthering Heights, The Cruel Sea, Love Is Eternal, Winter Wheat, Gone with the Wind, Bridge to the Sun, Three Came Home*—all these have something to say about love that cannot be learned from informational books.[2]

Too many adults wish to protect teenagers when they should be stimulating them to read of life as it is lived. When a story is true to life and well-written, the teenager will do well to arm himself with whatever experience such a book has to give him.

---

The section "Sex Isn't Necessary" was first published as "Mrs. Grundy, Go Home" in *Wilson Library Bulletin,* December 1958. *Ed.*

Once I was standing in the fiction department of my library when a teenage girl came up to ask about a novel she had heard of which dealt with homosexuality. A charming, well-bred woman patron who over-heard the request was aghast. She said, "I do not see why she wants to read that. I read it and found it very strong fare indeed." The girl and the woman had the same reason for reading the book—they wanted to know about this strange no-man's-land of sex. Adults need not look far for answers to their bewildered questions about teenagers' curiosity about sex. It is the same curiosity they once had and never quite outgrew.

The best books, old and new, have a richer and more subtle message about sex for the adolescent than he will hear from his peers. Certainly they will supplement whatever truths he may glean from a conscientious but sometimes tongue-tied parent.

All well-meaning adults and certainly all librarians want to "do right" by adolescents. I am one of those who was done right by, as many people would interpret the phrase. Brought up on a Texas cotton farm, I was protected from the evil world by two devout, educated, Presbyterian parents and a characterful grandmother, all eager to make me a lady, a Christian, and a good citizen. No intoxicants were allowed in our home, except when the doctor prescribed them for Grandmother in her old age, and then the bottle of whiskey was hidden in the back of a clothes cupboard and was not referred to by word or look. Since gamblers and toughs played cards, I had no association with them. Sex and dancing also seemed too closely connected to risk allowing me to sway to music in the arms of some panting male, so I didn't dance either. When a boy winked at me in the fifth grade, Mother told me not to wink back; as I grew older, I was told it would be perfectly all right to kiss a man after he had asked me to be his wife. Sex was *out*—out of our conversation and out of my reading matter.

From home I went to a college supported by our church and I graduated *summa cum laude—et puritate*.

After five years of teaching in little Texas towns, at twenty-six I betook myself, unsullied from the world, to Columbia University and a professional career in the East.

It took me ten years to become a normal human being. I beat off the men who tried to kiss me and was so unable to show the poor brutes affection that I would never have been married had not a kindly older man taught me, at forty, to love him. I had to learn that sex was normal and fulfilling, and that those who pervert or suspect it are pitiful. I wish that in my teens someone had given me *A Tree Grows in Brooklyn* to read, so I might have sympathized with "Sissy" rather than scorned her. I wish I had read *Of Human Bondage* earlier, for I was inhibited, too, and I needed to understand the effect of a love such as Philip had for Mildred.

Had I read *Ethan Frome* sooner, I might have lost any prim assurance that all one had to do was be good and characterful and one would be happy.

I desperately needed to have read the adult books that were kept from me, for I was not ready to cope with life and was merely amusing to people whom I wished to interest.

Of course, no one is reared so strictly any more, but even now too many adults would like to keep before adolescents only the good, the true, and the beautiful. Let them read of knights and ladies, of courage, of goodness. I agree; but I insist that we have a duty to teenagers that extends far beyond protection. We must be more positive than that. To become an adult citizen of America and the world requires an understanding of all sorts of people and the feelings that motivate them. It requires an acquaintance with people of all the other countries on the globe, and some conception of treating with them. It is important that young people read books that will help them meet these demands. It is a disservice to a young person, who must live dangerously, to acquaint him only with good, innocuous people in ideal situations.

Clifton Fadiman[3] has said that if a young person cannot understand what he reads, it will not harm him, while if he can understand what he reads, he is ready to read of life situations truly presented.

At what age are we to allow a young person to know of unpleasant things and sex? Many European libraries allow young people adult privileges at twenty-one. Is there some magic age at which one suddenly may be allowed to know of life, and shall we let this knowledge hit a youth at one fell blow?

Some adults honestly think average adolescents will understand when we tell them that they are not quite ready for the stories of adult experiences presented in serious fiction and that they will be content to wait. Like fun they will! Those with spirit will beat it out of the library to the nearest corner drugstore to inquire for the specific titles they have been refused, and to search there and in their friends' collections for juicier items. Theodore Roosevelt was told as a boy that he might not read Ouida.[4] Did he calmly accept the opinion of older wiser people? He did not. He read Ouida.

Young people mature at different rates of speed and many a teenager is better informed and more knowledgeable than the average adult. As he becomes interested in the adult world and its problems, he should not be recalled to more puerile interests and simplified writing. The readers' advisor for young adults should help the accelerated teenager find his way gradually among adult books, showing him how to develop critical ability, how to distinguish between sham and truth in writing, how to become acquainted with the great literary heritage that is his, so that when he finishes high school he will be already on the way to broadening his limited experience and enriching his understanding through adult books.

One swallow doesn't make a summer and one book will neither destroy nor save a reader—unless he is psychotic. It is the accumulation of a lifetime of reading that affects us for good or ill.

We heavy-footed adults might just as well slow down and let the black cat run. He will eventually win the race anyway—with no harm done.

# "Let the Lower Lights Be Burning"
## (*The Teenage Novel*)

Many of the young people in our cities are culturally deprived, trapped in a slough of frustration and despair. They have little understanding of what public property is. They have never sat down to a well-set table or heard an interesting conversation or known a father to love and respect. A resounding slap takes the place of a quiet discussion of good manners. They live in ghettos isolated from the mainstream of American life and their ideas are provincial in the extreme.

While the children of suburbia are more fortunate, many of them are also provincial. They do not see beyond their pretty little communities to the larger world or even to the slums of the nearby city. Surveys of suburbia usually agree that what the parents of these children want is two cars, membership in the country club, their children in private schools, and isolation from the problems of the poor. The children of both the ghetto and suburbia are living in a world growing constantly smaller of which they have very little understanding.

What can books do for these young people? Their most important contribution is to supplement experience, to intensify their lives. However long these young people may live, most of them will know few months or years that are filled with meaning. They will experience few passionate love affairs, few victories, few overwhelming griefs, few moments of insight and inspiration. Without books, they can live and die naively innocent of so much experience. But the young person who reads can live a thousand years and a thousand lives. In a few hours, at any time, he can add to his meager experience another whole lifetime condensed to its meaningful moments, with all the dull, uneventful days left out. He can go back in time three hundred years before Christ to travel with Theseus in *The King Must Die*, dancing on the backs of

---

"Let the Lower Lights Be Burning" was first published in *English Journal*, November 1957. *Ed.*

charging bulls, threading the labyrinth to slay the minotaur, and winning Ariadne's love. He can learn what it means to be consumed by a dream when he reads of Jesse Stuart,[5] Moss Hart, Gordon Parks, and Agnes de Mille. He can experience the overwhelming passion of Anna Karenina, weep over Anne Frank or George's anguish for Lennie. He can understand the poignancy of living from *Our Town* and struggle with bewildered Holden Caulfield to adjust dreams to harsh reality. But why go on? Here in books is life a thousand times more various and richer than anyone could ever live it.

Books are literary atom bombs capable of destroying stupidity, cant, insularity, and prejudice—if they are read. The trouble is that not enough people read books at any time, and so the ideas contained in them, like our supply of bombs, are stockpiled. One reason for this is that we have killed off many young readers by our determination to give them only great books too complex and deep for younger, inexperienced readers to fully understand. We should first teach the youngest teenagers, who have limited imaginations and scanty experience, to love to read, and this can be done by giving them books they can thoroughly enjoy—teenage novels, for instance.

At the appearance of teenage novels the literary critics went into tailspins and vied with each other in expressing their scorn. Some librarians agreed with them, while others who have read and circulated these books and listened to the reactions of young readers have come to believe that the public library can make good use of teenage novels: to teach the apathetic the love of reading; to satisfy some of the adolescent's emotional and psychological needs; to throw light on the problems of adolescence; to explore the teenager's relationship to his community; and to lead him to adult reading.

## To Teach the Apathetic the Love of Reading

People who read books are enigmas to some young people. They wonder why anyone would withdraw from the hurly-burly of the street where he can converse with people to go off alone with a book. These adolescents have no interest in distant places, interplay of character, or man's struggle against fate. The girls are interested in growing up and dating; the boys like sports, space travel, cars, adventure— whatever affords an entree to a man's world.

If a younger girl whose friends are unread speaks of going to the library because she loves to read good books, she may arouse only concern for her eccentricity, but on the other hand, if she shows her friends that she is returning *Seventeenth Summer* by Maureen Daly and *Double Date* [1952] by Rosamond Du Jardin, it is quite likely that one or more of her nonreading friends will look these books over, listen to her warm recommendations of them, and return with her to borrow them from the library. Moreover, these girls will tell others about them and constantly increase the number of younger teenager patrons of the library.

A teenage boy is quite likely to be intrigued by the science-fiction novels his friend is reading when he looks at the jackets portraying ant men, robots controlled by the laws of robotics, a spaceship buried in a sea of moon dust, humanoids, hive-hearts, men from Mars. Though a boy may be a reluctant reader, if he reads one of these stories, he will find that writers of science fiction can take the earthbound on flights of fancy to distant planets and out into the incredible void. Outrageous as some of these plots may sound, they are the fairy tales of this techno-logical age and they intrigue readers because no one can prove they are impossible. If we had been told a quarter of a century ago that children might vacation on the moon or that mankind would possess the instruments of its own destruction, who would have given credence to such wild tales? *The Three Musketeers* and *Moby Dick* are better literature than science fiction, but they do not lure the nonreader to make a first contact with the library.

If there is one subject dear to teenage boys, it is automobiles. All of them either own their own cars or hot rods or dream of owning them. In Felsen's *Hot Rod*, one of the earliest stories on the subject, Bud Crayne's race with the policeman, his insolent attitude that brakes are only for sissies, and the results of his folly make a story beloved by boys despite the obvious lesson driven home at the end. They like stories that go into some detail about mechanical problems. They want the feel of driving an MG or a Jaguar with their tremendous power, remarkable maneuverability, and manner of burning up the track in the big races. There is also a great need for stories of motorcycles.

Few teenage novels will ever be classics, but they speak to young people in a language they can understand on subjects that interest them. For that reason they are bait for reluctant readers. Unless the adolescent can be convinced that reading is fun and that he must make time for it in his busy life, he will never become a reader. No books accomplish this more quickly for the masses of younger teenagers than teenage novels.

## To Satisfy the Adolescent's Emotional and Psychological Needs

Why does a teenage girl rush to the telephone after school to call up the friends she saw all day and with whom she rode home on the bus a little while ago? Why does she talk for hours and hours on the only telephone in the house? Why does she giggle so much? Why is she such a pain in the neck? Because she so desperately wants to be popular. She must find out how to be attractive to boys before old age overtakes her. She is only six or seven short years from twenty, when old age sets in, and if she does not succeed in being alluring, she may end up as a "brain" with a career and never know the meaning of love or have children or anything! She is so beset by her own worries and fears that she is often callous to the rights and privileges of others and indifferent to the advantages of a really good education or the charm of culture. However, in the midst of her feverish turmoil, she will go to the library and borrow teenage romances.

The warmest defender of these stories would not recommend them for the Great Books list nor ask to be marooned with them on a desert island, but they do have their good points. They are as wholesome as oatmeal and they are invaluable standards of taste for the girl whose association with boys consists in gathering with the crowd at the corner drugstore and engaging in friendly pushing and shoving. These teenage romances give younger inexperienced girls a glimpse of the dating world, of good manners, of fitting into one's family circle with respect and affection.

The adolescent is just discovering the appalling fact adults know all too well—that we are all essentially lonely. He has an idea that his unformed worries and fears, as well as those clearly defined, are peculiar to him. In these simple little stories he welcomes the discovery that what he thought were his individual problems are common ones that other teenagers have met and solved. He takes courage and makes a quicker and better adjustment. There is yet another psychological factor to be noted here. The technical term for it is probably "wish-fulfillment." The more awkward and shy and unglamorous a girl is, the more interest she may have in reading about a girl who is the embodiment of what she herself wishes to be. Certainly a steady diet of stories of happy people leading happy lives may dull the senses over a long period of time, but a few books of this type may be no more harmful than the child's fairy tales if the individual's reading is directed eventually to a more balanced realism.

## To Throw Light on the Problems of Adolescence

Besides the difficulties of growing up and learning to get along with one's family and peers, other problems are dealt with that may not seem so important to adults but are crucial to adolescents. Modern authors of teenage stories have depicted skillfully the girl whose lovable father is an alcoholic, the girl suddenly faced with the fact that her parents do not love each other and that her warm circle of love is an illusion. There is the father coming home from prison, the mother who wants people to think she and her daughter are like sisters and who is always the star with both the boys and girls among her shy daughter's friends. We read of the compulsive eater, the basketball player sensitive about his height, the "select-girls-school" type who learns that the protection her family's wealth has given her has also made her a snob. And again and again there is the study of values between the glitter and the gold of which Mary Stolz's *Pray Love, Remember* [1954] is probably the best. In this story Dody Jenks escaped from her dull life and prosaic family to glamorous Oyster Bay and a rich household for whose little boy she was responsible. Strange to tell, the Oyster Bay family wasn't much better than her own and Dody's sense of values was confused until a Jewish boy with whom she fell in love showed her, before he died, how to measure life's intangibles and to attain inner strength.

For the boys, sports stories often deal with the importance of subordinating one's desire to be a star to the good of the team and frequently the relative importance of winning and playing fair is weighed.

## To Explore the Teenager's Relationship to His Community

One of the first teenage novels to deal with the boy and girl who "had to get married," Felsen's *Two and the Town* [1952], shook up conservative librarians. What happened wasn't any more Buff's fault than Elaine's. It just happened. The two respectable middle-class families saw that the children were respectably married and sent them off on a pseudo-honeymoon. The boy's resentment at losing a chance to play college football, the girl's embarrassment at being asked by the school principal not to come back to school, and the coming of the baby are skillfully handled, and though the ending holds out hope that the boy may grow up to his responsibilities, the beating the two took for a year or more would surely dismay any adolescent.

The book came off the press in the fifties, a few weeks before the American Library Association met in New York City. There was to be a preconference on young-adult work in the public library, and I was to sit on a panel where I expected the book to be questioned. I immediately bought a copy for each young-adult branch collection in the Pratt system with the request that each librarian give it to a teenager to read and get his honest reaction. One of the librarians said he gave it to a boy whose mother charged into the branch one evening to ask, "Did you give this book to my boy?" The librarian was looking for a hole to crawl into when the woman explained that she, the boy, and the boy's friend had read and discussed it. She thought it really very good, but only for boys as mature and well read as her son. (Parents often think their children are superior to the herd.)

All the reactions from young people had been favorable, and I set out for the ALA panel meeting. Sure enough, *Two and the Town* came up for discussion and the panel seemed agreed it "was not up to Felsen," which simply meant they thought it too hot to handle. I came to the book's defense saying we had no other book that dealt honestly with this problem, which was of interest and concern to teenagers, and asked what they would give a young person who wanted a book on this subject. One of the true-blue ladies drew herself up and announced, "I would give him *The Scarlet Letter!*"

Times have changed and most librarians accept such books as a matter of course. One of the best is *Mr. and Mrs. Bo Jo Jones* [1968] by Head. Here the death of the baby makes it possible for the two families to engineer an annulment of the marriage, but it also brings the boy and girl together in grief and gives them a realization of the true meaning of marriage.

Years ago John Tunis undertook to show the workings of democracy through sports stories and succeeded admirably. Many sports stories today depict the sports-crazy town that cries for the blood of the coach who loses, whatever the justification, and deal with prejudice against Negro, Jewish, and foreign players.

All sorts of problems that bother teenagers are dealt with in contemporary teenage novels. Many adolescents who are worried about matters they hesitate to discuss find what they are looking for in teenage stories. Most of these are adequately written; they are neither pornographic nor Communistic, they hurt no one, and they afford a great deal of pleasure to a lot of young people.[6]

## To Lead the Teenager to Adult Reading

The problem in the library world is not teenage novels but the librarian who allows them to become ends in themselves and fails to make use of them as simple, effective tools in the development of readers. Teenage stories should not be shelved as a collection in themselves, since this tends to develop dead-end readers. They should be shelved with adult books for teenagers and not represent over 20 percent of the titles in the collection. The librarian should know his readers and books well enough to be able to introduce readable, appealing adult titles at the propitious time and see that the young reader gradually moves into adult reading with all the enthusiasm he once had for teenage stories.

In America provision must be made for gifted students, but the public schools and the public library are rightly committed to the enlightenment of the masses. If the masses are to recognize demagogues as they arise, if they are to vote as individuals instead of as city blocks under the rule of a political boss, if they are to understand the problems of this country and its role in world affairs, they need to avail themselves of the wisdom in books. Certainly teenage novels will not solve the world's problems, but if they lead more people to a first understanding of the pleasures and profits to be found in print, they have a place in the reading program.

# ❦ VI ❦

# Fighting Weeds and Insects

## The Strange Device . . . *"Excelsior!"*

Some years ago I went for my summer vacation to the Poconos and put up at a summer hotel. On one Sunday evening of "my week" a young minister came up to hold vesper services. After two hymns and a prayer he spoke briefly, presenting the hardships of the Christian life and explaining that he had given up "the world" and its temptations to preach the Gospel. As I looked at this overly earnest young man, I wondered how much deprivation he was suffering. Had he remained in "the world," would he be dancing down the primrose path, clinking glasses, and tempting pretty ladies? I also did not like his attitude toward his profession. The ministry is surely more than denial and hardship, and he was probably doing better financially than if he had hit Wall Street. I should have respected him more had he taken pride in the ministry and spoken more of fulfillment and less of denial. All in all, I got a meager blessing from the vesper service.

Why do people go into the professions? Because they want to. Most intelligent college graduates have to choose between business and the professions. Those who elect to enter the business world want the position and security money can give them. They are interested in the world of commerce, are well suited to it, and are willing to work hard for what they want. It is to their credit and better for all of us if they enter the business world.

Other young people elect to go into the professions because they wish to work with people and ideas. They cannot find rich fulfillment in the business world and feel their modicum of financial reward is compensated for by the personal enrichment they receive from professional life. They honestly want to bear through snow and ice a banner with the strange device "Excelsior."[1]

Unfortunately, the public generally has the impression that librarians are not so interested in carrying the banner as in getting out of the snow and ice to find a warm place. I believe this is because we are more technicians than professionals. Our activities center largely around manipulating book collections and buildings and staffs so that queries can be answered. We stress skills and the performance of them rather than our relationship to the individuals these skills are supposed to help. If the day ever comes, as it surely will, when computers answer questions related to schoolwork and most other general inquiries, the public library can be set up like chain stores with a general manager, one or two assistants, and clerks to put the books in order on the shelves.

Most professions center their activities around the individual. When misfortune strikes a home, the minister is often notified. He comes with sympathy to hold one's hand and say a little prayer, attempting by word and look to soften the blow. Many a teacher has so identified with his individual students that he has increased their vision and changed their entire lives for the better. Clifton Fadiman said that in John Erskine's class one did not so much learn something as become something.[2] The lawyer enters into the personal life of his client to see that he receives justice. We love and trust the physician as our personal protection against pain and death. The librarian, more often than not, is impersonal. So while other professions, centered as they are on the individual, must fill their ranks with personalities strong enough to win confidence and persuade people to go along with them, the library profession can absorb numbers of colorless personalities so long as they can organize and administer a book collection and reply to the questions of the few patrons who approach them.

The library profession hopes to improve its image and seems to feel this can be done by proof of efficiency. We even set up workshops on the operation of computers. Library schools train for efficiency, as is witnessed by their catalogs listing page after page of courses in descriptive cataloging, subject cataloging and classification, advanced classification, indexing and abstracting, automation of library services, reference and bibliography, advanced reference and bibliography, government documents, research, administration, principles of book selection, and one or two electives on materials for children, and rarely, adolescents. Over half of the required courses are not really necessary for public and school librarians. In place of those that could be eliminated, the schools might set up courses designed to train students in the promotion of reading among people of all ages and types, and in the meantime, make readers of the library-school students themselves.

A survey of the Baltimore-Washington metropolitan libraries showed that half the patrons of the public library had come to it simply for a good book to read.[3] The general public, even the unread portion of it, has a deep and abiding faith in the moving power of the book. The public is so sure books are dynamite that they often burn those they believe to be evil to keep people from falling under their spells. Yet patrons who come to the library are seldom accosted by a librarian who has thought enough of books to read very many of them, or if he has read extensively, cares enough to recommend books to others searching for good reading.

The library-school graduate often lacks a professional attitude. He is inclined to think he has learned what he needs to know and is now ready to fill a professional position. He really is ready to perform fairly well as a technician, but in young-adult work he is sadly lacking, for as a rule, he does not know books nor has he been taught how to work with people. Furthermore, he does not feel he should be asked to remedy these deficiencies on his own time.

How often I have been asked why the library does not provide time for reading in the daily schedule and not ask the assistant to read books at night. A new assistant, duly certified by a library school, felt the required outside reading under my administration was an imposition, at least when he first learned of it, though he was at a loss to answer such simple requests as for a story about the American Revolution that was easy to read. He complained to his branch librarian, who sometimes came to my office to plead for these new people, reminding me they "were so young" and should be having a good time. I do not know any other profession where people expect to work eight hours a day and always have the remainder of their time free. Ministers comfort the bereaved and bury the dead on their days off; doctors answer emergency calls day and night; lawyers work extra hours to prepare briefs; and teachers grade papers and make lesson plans almost every night. A professional is not a blue-collar worker who punches a clock. He works when he is needed and he renews himself constantly. This renewal by reading is generally overlooked by librarians, old and young.

Some years ago I was very ill in the Johns Hopkins Hospital. Since I could not sleep well at night, the young intern assigned to our ward usually called on me around midnight to chat a while and lift my spirits before he went off duty. The next morning at six o'clock I would see him walking briskly through the halls, half dead but going strong. One morning while he stood by my bed, almost asleep on his feet, I stormed, "The Hopkins Hospital should be ashamed. It has hundreds of applicants for internships from all over the world yet it takes only a few interns and works them to death. They should take at least twice as many and not treat you this way." He took me up quickly to say, "Oh no! That way I wouldn't see as many cases!" This was a professional dedicated to perfecting himself to serve people, even at the cost of physical suffering. I could not help thinking of those nice young assistants who were so unhappy at being asked to read books. It is my belief that the young-adult librarian's love of people can be measured by the amount of reading he is willing to do for them.

When the time comes that library schools train readers' advisors as well as technicians; when administrators make the promotion of reading as important as the informational services; when staff members render creative professional service to individuals, we shall not have to worry about our image.

# YA—The Library Bastard

According to the Baltimore-Washington metropolitan survey mentioned previously, 50 per cent of the patrons who come to the public library have in mind only a good book to read. Now, these people are a problem, as so many of them like to read fiction—which might run the circulation figures for fiction higher than those for nonfiction, thus leaving the impression that the library's patrons are not "serious" readers. It would never do to have more people reading for enjoyment and enrichment than for information. If this should happen, it will not be the fault of the librarian, who seldom calls attention to fiction but stresses educational reading with such displays as "Know Your State" or "Understanding Missiles." The fiction collection, dealing as it does with the emotions and feelings of people, is a kind of literary bastard since it does not fit into the library's philosophy of educating oneself by "serious" reading.

But the biggest bastard in the library family is the young-adult department. The work in this department cannot be done by technicians or colorless people. It is centered around service to and enrichment of the individual. Its pedigree reads: "*Out* of service to the individual *by* the promotion of reading." This sire and dam are not fully recognized in the library's stud books and their offspring has been disowned in some quarters. It is time we reexamined the bastard's relation to the family to determine his eligibility for recognition. Here I serve as his advocate.

My assistants and I believed that we should attempt through books to take each individual, whatever his reading level, and develop him to his full potential as a reader, widening his interests and deepening his understanding until he came to know that he was a member of one race—the human race—and a citizen of one planet—the earth. This was a big undertaking and required highly developed professional skill. It would have been impossible to have implemented our goals by simply shelving books in order and letting young people browse around. It required on the part of the assistants a very rich reading background, sincere liking for teenagers, energy, dedication, and mastery of the art of interesting young people in reading. They had to become real people with hearts open to experience and minds capable of absorbing it. They were warned against becoming like the two little librarians who share an apartment and go into hiding from the city.

These two typical little librarians waste hours sharing their limited experiences and bemoaning the scarcity of men. For entertainment they go to dinner at the apartment of two other little librarians, where they discuss the queer characters that come into the library every day, their most effective methods of squelching troublemakers, and the breakdown of the charging machine. And they bemoan the scarcity of men.

This kind of isolation from the community is like sitting alone at a gourmet banquet eating crackers and milk. In every community, large or small, there are intelligent, stimulating people interested in living. They race horses, take part in politics, join little theater groups, grow roses, paint, watch birds, hike, swim, play tennis, work with the League of Women Voters, raise funds for the symphony orchestra, and so on. No librarian has time for all these activities but he or she should be interested in at least one of them and get to know people who are concerned with something beside the breakdown of the charging machine. Too many librarians are anemic. When their library joins the blood bank, it is difficult to find enough donors with sufficient iron in their blood to renew the strength of the least-depleted donor. This anemia may be the result of holing up in that little apartment.

By his performance on the floor of the library, the librarian leaves a very good impression with patrons of the kind of person he is. Too often the patron in the library sees the librarian sensibly dressed, seated, earnestly sorting cards or reading. If someone gets up enough courage to ask him a question, he looks up patiently and says "Yes?" Or if there is noise, he raps on the desk and stares down the offenders. If the noise continues, he yells "QUIET!" This does not "send" teenagers—or anyone else.

From left to right, Margaret's sister, Helen, her mother, Hadena Alexander, and Margaret at Seven Falls in South Cheyenne Canyon, Colorado.

The book wagon in the first year of circulating books in the streets of Baltimore, ca 1943.

Edwards and her assistant checking out books to neighborhood young people, ca 1944.

The Bell Ringers Booth at the first book fair for YAs at Pratt, 1951.

Pratt book fairs were given for every senior English class in every public high school in Baltimore, ca 1951–1955.

Pratt YA librarians at an annual gathering at Edwards' farm, 'Ed Ache, where they all performed skits and put on "roasts," ca 1952.

Edwards on tractor, sometime in the early sixties.

On the day of her retirement, October 9, 1962, Edwards
greets staff and friends in her office.

For a retirement gift, the staff decided to go big. They purchased a bull from Nicholas Merryman's farm. But Bullie Sol Edwards did not perform as Edwards had hoped, so Mr. Merryman gave her a new one—called "Pappy," after Hemingway—who did very well and increased the herd.

Edwards in the door of the hay loft at 'Ed Ache, ca October 1963.

Phillip "Doc" Edwards, ca 1965.

Annie Oakley takes aim at a nest of blade snakes in an enormous oak tree at 'Ed Ache to the amusement of children and adult guests at a picnic, during the late sixties.

Edwards and Emerson Greenaway in Pratt's central hall at
the celebration of the 100th birthday of Pratt, fall 1986.

Season's Greetings

Tammy Faye, Fawn
Hall and Me

The 1986 or 1987 Christmas card from 'Ed Ache. Edwards with
Tammy Faye and Fawn Hall.

Margaret Alexander Edwards
October 1902–April 1988

When patrons are in the library, especially if they are young adults, the well-dressed, well-groomed librarian should be up on his feet, looking friendly and approachable. Think how impatient we become when we stand in a shop waiting for a clerk to assist us. When teenagers come to the library after school the librarian should move about among them, helping old customers and making friends with new people. As one high-school girl put it, the relation of a librarian to young adults should be that of a hostess to house guests. This girl went on to say that a gracious hostess would not tell her guests provisions are in the refrigerator, assuming they know how to cook and can prepare their own meals. Emily Post says good manners are based on common sense and kindness of heart. These are the same guidelines a young-adult librarian might follow in establishing good relations with teenagers.

We should have enough faith in ourselves and enthusiasm for books and people to make the initial contact rather than leaving it to the insecure, often inarticulate, young person. By our social grace and tact we should set all young people at ease and make their trips to the library an experience they look forward to and enjoy. This same grace and tact will lead us to let alone the youngster who wishes to be let alone to help himself. But most adolescents are so overwhelmed at the sight of all those shelves holding hundreds of books written by authors they never heard of that help from someone who does know is more than welcome. It is good to have a friend at court who will go to great lengths to help one with a difficult problem and who keeps smiling, no matter how rough the going gets.

In our monthly meetings we seldom reviewed new books. When twenty or so new titles had been read by the assistants, they were assembled in one place with written reviews attached and each assistant looked them over and made his purchases. This left the meetings free for more important matters. We studied how to interest reluctant readers as well as the accelerated college-bound students. We decided what positions we would take on controversial books of interest to young people. We planned programs to feature reliable books of sex information for teenagers who were getting their knowledge of sex in back alleys. We viewed and discussed films and constantly evaluated the effectiveness of our special projects such as book fairs, school visits, the young-adult program for which we were responsible on a rock 'n roll radio station, or our book-reviewing publication by and for teenagers. When an assistant discovered a new approach that seemed effective, we shared the idea, and if there were doubts about it, we did some experimenting.

Not every assistant was a howling success with the young people, but most of them were. They did not impinge on the privacy of teenagers or oversell them. Teenagers crowded around them after school and it was evident that they held the affection and respect of their clientele. Many a mother who read in the young-adult department as a high-school girl has dropped in to tell about her children and to say she hopes that when they are older someone will make reading as meaningful for them as it was made for her.

And yet I was told by the dean of a library school, and I have heard administrators and staff members say the same thing with assurance, that any staff member can help young adults just as well as a special assistant. I never saw a general assistant who had the background or understanding to work as effectively with young adults as did my trained assistants. Of course, he can do as well if we define the word "help" to mean operating as a technician, i.e., if a girl asks for a romance, tell her to look under "Romance" in the catalog or give her the H. W. Wilson *Standard Catalog for High School Libraries.* If she persists in asking what the books are about, she can be shown the annotations in library references. Few assistants untrained in young-adult work can satisfy teenagers who ask, "Will you find me two real good love stories?" "What is *Mr. and Mrs. Bo Jo Jones* about?" "Will you help me find a real thin little book about going West?" "I loved this book. Will you get me one like it?" "Would you be willing to speak at our assembly next month?" "My teacher said to ask you if *Manchild in the Promised Land* has been approved for high-school reading." "My teacher sent this note to you. She is coming in Saturday morning to ask you to help her bring up to date the unit our ninth grade class has on 'The Lure of the Middle Ages.' "

Young people often feel the need to talk about the books they have read. They will express themselves freely only to those librarians they trust to help them pursue an awakened interest. A general assistant could not possibly attend to his other duties and read widely enough in this field to function effectively.

Many administrators disband YA collections to make room for more "serious" adult reading. In serving young people it seems to me important to keep together those books most essential to the introduction of adult reading. This collection serves the same time-saving purpose as the ready reference collection in the reference room. There are a few hundred books that are used so much that it is a waste of time to run over the library constantly searching for them. Also, when the young-adult librarian is away from the library it is a great help to the youngster to know there is one place in the library where he is pretty sure to find something he will like to read.

When administrators eliminate YA work they usually compliment themselves by saying, "We treat the teenagers just as we do the adults."

I'll say they do. They make it possible for the teenagers to join the 84 per cent of all adults who never speak to the librarian, who have learned to shift for themselves whether they know their way around or not, and who can always rely on the catalog for advice and inspiration.

In winding up my case I admit that under the prevailing standards of public librarianship the bastard YA cannot claim legitimate membership in the library family, but the fault is with the system, not with the bastard. As long as public librarianship is concerned primarily with collecting and making available information and educational materials, it seems arbitrary to ask a college graduate to take another year off and spend a large sum of money to get another degree in order to learn to perform little better than he would if he were trained on the job. Since trained librarians have been in such short supply, many a large public library has been forced to employ untrained college graduates and in the process has learned that they are quite acceptable without a B.S. or A.M. degree in Library Science. Administrators keep this secret well and insist that promising people leave to get a degree, for they know this union card is essential for advancement to the big money and the big jobs and they also wish to keep alive the idea that librarians belong to a profession in which extra training is necessary. In some large libraries thought is being given to employing trained heads and supervisors and filling all other positions with staff who will be trained on the job.

Many a library-board member thinks it is folly to pay high salaries to library-school graduates when they do not see librarians who have been so trained doing anything that seems too difficult for any intelligent college graduate to learn. However, if they saw trained librarians up out of their chairs and on the floor, sought after by young and old, handing out books and discussing them with people; if their children came home from high school excited about books the public librarian had described to their class, or had in their hands attractive book lists and were saying what it meant to go to the library and find a friendly expert who knew just the kind of books one would love to read—then a board member might conclude that special training was worth paying for. But before this happens, public libraries will have to change their philosophy and library schools their curricula.

If, however, we continue to confine ourselves to administering collections, to making information and materials available, to answering questions but remaining unconcerned for the individual, then we should be honest enough to admit we are technicians, cease insisting on professional status, disown the bastard YA, and catch up with our work. After all, we librarians are not to blame that Americans are the worst-read people of the world's democracies . . . or are we?

Once a young man named Moses who was herding sheep in the Egyptian desert looked up and saw a burning bush and, "Behold, the bush burned with fire and the bush was not consumed." When he turned aside to investigate, a voice called to him out of the bush and said, "Put off thy shoes from thy feet, for the place whereon thou standest is holy ground." Many administrators and librarians wander about in the desert and never look up to see the miraculous burning bush. Instead they devote their attention to taking care of the sheep, a useful occupation, but it was the voice from the burning bush that inspired Moses to lead his people from the bondage of Egypt to the Promised Land.

## The City Kid and the Library

During the last of the four summers when I was sweating out a library degree, I was slated for a seminar in library administration that I was sure would kill me. So I borrowed the notes of a fellow librarian who had previously taken the course, read them over on the train, took the exam, and got a C. This enabled me to enroll for the same number of points in the adjoining university, where I took an exciting course in philosophy—a symposium introduced by Morris Cohen.[4] This was before World War II, when I and other innocents believed that despite a few slips, man was climbing the ladder rung by rung from the lowly earth to the vaulted skies. Morris Cohen said this was not so. Man was getting neither better and better nor worse and worse, but as the individual had his ups and downs with some good days and some not so good, so the race maintained something of a norm.

If this is so, is it not as true for teenagers as for others? As a group, are they basically different from what they always were? Socrates said the teenagers of his day were simply impossible. Two thousand years later the young people of my generation were enthusiastic over the theory of companionate marriage. They drank bathtub gin from girls' slippers, whispered over Elinor Glyn's *A Bed of Roses*, and sang "The Sheik of Araby" with deep emotion while their mothers tore the buttons off Lawrence Tibbett's clothes.[5]

Certainly some teenagers do terrible things today, but it is quite likely that Morris Cohen was right—that basically man does not change. Man's activities may fall into new patterns, his conception of the world and the universe will be as new each year as the discoveries

---

"The City Kid and the Library" was first published in *Top of the News*, November 1967, 62–71. *Ed.*

of science, his habits of work and play will be altered by electronics, but his concerns will remain constant. He will still need love and security, he will still seek for identity and fulfillment, he will still wonder about the meaning of his own and all existence. Though he may die without realizing it, the answers to many of his questions are in books. It is especially important that the adolescent learn this, for his search for meanings is especially intense.

All over the world young people are interested in politics and society's welfare. But their eagerness to take up causes and protest, their readiness to overthrow the established order and set right what seems to them wrong, their potential power in sheer numbers, mean they desperately need a sound attitude toward life, civilized feelings, an understanding of people and cultures. They need something to go on besides emotion. There are various sources where they may find understanding, ideas, and enrichment, but the most reliable, never-failing source is the books on the shelves of the public library.

What is the public library doing to interest adolescents in reading these books? In too many cases, nothing.

Generally, librarians have been content to supply factual material and technical help, but this is not the case in some cities where provision is made for the adolescent and special services are offered. Detroit has conducted programs for young adults on TV for years with success; Philadelphia has worked with delinquents and probationers; Dallas and Seattle have worked effectively with schools; New York City has led the way in work with manual-minded vocational students; Boston, Pittsburgh, St. Louis, Los Angeles, and other cities have set up special services for young adults, while Baltimore in addition to its program in the schools has been an innovator with new ideas such as book fairs, in-service training, and at present, experimental programs in the war on poverty. Other cities I have not mentioned are also doing good work, I am sure, but the present social crisis in our big cities calls for a general breakthrough. It is extremely important that city kids all over the nation find out that the public library has a lot more to offer them than material for school assignments. Because this is so very urgent I am going to make five charges against the public library, not in a spirit of hostility or carping criticism, but with a firm faith in the potential of the public library for influencing the thinking and feeling of the adolescent. By pointing out what seem to me to be failings, I may stimulate thinking on new courses of action. I should like to cite as state's evidence for the charges I shall make the recent *Survey of Metropolitan Public Library Users of Maryland Baltimore-Washington Metropolitan Area* by Mary Lee Bundy, Associate Professor of the University of Maryland School of Library and Information Services. The urban district surveyed is organized, supported, and patronized well enough to seem as representative, up-to-date, fair an example as we might find of the city library we are here discussing.

## How Has the Public Library Failed the City Teenager?

*1. It has failed in the relationship of the majority of the staff to adolescents. (Young-adult librarians and those innately gracious staff members are not included here.)*

The ALA Ad Hoc Committee on Instruction in the Use of Libraries in the report it presented at the San Francisco Conference in 1967 made this statement: "One of the greatest blocks to the total use of public libraries has been the attitude of generations of public librarians toward students." The Bundy survey cited above shows that though adults were not unusually critical of the staff, 25 per cent of the students complained. One said, "I appreciate the librarians who can tell when you need help and offer it to you in a pleasant manner without making you feel ignorant." Another wrote, "Kindness is a virtue and I hope in the future we will have kinder librarians."

For years I have attempted to figure out why so many librarians dislike teenagers. Is it that these librarians are insecure and feel there is more status in working with adults? Are they afraid of adolescents? Is it a little touch of sadism that leads a librarian to humiliate the defenseless young person, bawling him out for a stupid assignment his teacher gave him, interrogating him in a seemingly polite way that undermines his confidence? Though adolescents make up about half our patronage outside the children's department, many librarians still consider them an interruption to business. It is not only the 25 per cent who write out complaints who resent the staff. Even those not mis-treated resent seeing librarians bully-rag their friends. Yet we wonder why there is such a shortage of librarians and put out more attractive recruiting material to explain to these young people what an oppor-tunity for service librarianship affords.

*2. The urban public library is off-balance. Its concern is with its informational services to the neglect of other needs of its patrons.*

Since the simultaneous explosions of scientific knowledge and the population, all hands have been put to work to get the facts to the people as expeditiously as possible and to deal with the never-ending, ever-broadening school assignments. Some cities have eliminated young-adult work above the ninth grade and have transferred positions calling for special skills in introducing reading to the adolescent to more utilitarian uses. Some cities have kept token YA work, assigning the head of young-adult work to a subsidiary position and regarding this specialization as a kind of extravagance. Most administrators cannot see why capable librarians should be talking about books and reading to teenagers when several students are waiting for material on the mineral resources of Hawaii. Even those administrators who believe in the promotion of reading have no system for promoting outstanding young librarians in this field except to remove them from their specialty and make them branch librarians. The money is in administration rather than in the promotion of reading. It should be in both. With our microfilm, indices, teletypes, catalogs, and impersonal staffs, the machine is truly our message and for high-school students it is also a massage.[6] Yet according to the survey cited above, the percentage of people who come to the library for general reading is exactly the same as that of those who come for materials or information on a subject. So our services are geared to the needs of half the patrons who come to the library.

One day during the summer when I drove the horse-drawn vegetable cart loaded with books through the streets of a Baltimore slum I pulled up in front of a hovel where a Negro mother was ironing. Her little boy wanted to borrow a book and when I showed him a fairy tale we were ready to clinch the deal. But first I called to the mother, "Is it all right to let Henry have a book?" She looked very doubtful but eventually said, "You can let him have a book if you give him something that will do him good." She meant I could give him a speller or an arithmetic book, but the fairy tale was out. Her philosophy of reading is shared by many librarians.

*3. The public library is passive rather than active.*

The Bundy survey asks, "In all the areas it attempts to cover, is the library's role a passive supplying one or should it undertake active programs and services of its own?" As far as the adolescent is concerned, it is time the public library answered this question. Do we or do we not believe that it is important enough for teenagers to read books that it behooves us to bestir ourselves and not lay the problem entirely in the laps of other institutions? Polls and surveys tell us what we already know, that adolescents do very little unassigned reading. Are public libraries willing to let it go at that?

Once I was walking through the exhibits at a librarians' conference and my eye happened to fall on a panel in a booth where I read, "The time has come for the library to recognize that its primary responsibility today is to the other agencies of society and only secondarily to the individual who walks through the doors."

It seems this was a quotation from a talk made by someone in the book world. If this view is widely held, we will become the only profession not concerned primarily with the individual. Does it not follow that when we agree to this, we will cease to be a profession and become the warehouse of other professions?

We run too many of our libraries like Helpy-Selfy supermarkets. You put it in the basket, we check it out. As a result, the adolescent often arrives at the checking-out point with an empty basket or with a book he selected by its title or cover, which may turn out to be a bad bargain. The Bundy survey says 47 per cent of the library's patrons leave without being completely satisfied. At present, librarians generally believe that if books are in order on the shelves, the reader in search of a good book to read has been served. If he needs help, let him ask. The supermarket, the automat, and libraries are agreed on this method. Many other institutions that serve the public and believe in their product put skilled salespeople on the floor, not behind desks filing cards or reading book reviews and waiting for the customer to approach them.

A short while ago I was teaching a course on the adolescent and his reading in a well-known library school. I was lecturing the students on the fine art of floor work when one of them said, "Mrs. Edwards, I am confused. You speak of what you call floor work as if it were a generally accepted practice. In all my life I never had a librarian approach me and suggest a book I might like to read." I was horrified and asked the class if any of them had also never been approached by a librarian, and all but four raised their hands. I have taught courses in three library schools and held workshops over the country for many summers. With each group, I would ask how many were ever approached by a librarian with a reading suggestion after they outgrew the children's department, and as a rule, two or three hands would go up. Often students would drop by the desk after class to say how they went to libraries for years without a glimmer of recognition, let alone a suggestion for reading from a librarian. They remember this with resentment. One of my students, reared in a large midwestern city, said, "I remember getting my adult card. When my juvenile card expired and I went to renew it, the clerk asked my age, said I was old enough now for an adult card, and gave me one. No one suggested where to begin reading in this alien land." How can it be possible that librarians would not wish to share their pleasure in reading? How could they not help talking about books to patrons? Yet in city after city public librarians have not suggested an enjoyable book to a single teenager. The Bundy survey says, "In the day-to-day operation of a library, librarians talk to only a small number of users." And again,

"The library user is apparently on his own; only 16 per cent sought help from a staff member." (And we can be sure many of those who contacted the librarian lived to regret it.) The machine is our message.

The promotion of reading calls for intensive, skillful training. Most library schools ignore this field or give it the once-over lightly in favor of training research technicians. The training is in library science rather than in the art of librarianship. This makes sense because college and special libraries want this kind of training for their employees. For that matter, that is the type of librarian most in demand in public libraries. If library schools turned out specialists in the promotion of reading, they might have difficulty placing them. Incidentally, this is the basis of many complaints about library-school training. Those students who enter the library profession because they love books and wish to work with people soon discover they are being trained for technical services and become bored and disillusioned. But readers' advisers can be developed by in-service training if the administrator believes in the service and if he has a staff member who knows books, likes people, and is an inspiring supervisor. To be honest, isn't the root of our passivity the fact that so many librarians do not read books outside their own interests and do not like people?

*4. Our obsession with the catalog is a boomerang that has sailed back to harm our relations with the teenager and to diminish his joy in reading.*

I hesitate to make this fourth charge for it is heresy and is likely to end once and for all my activities in the library world, but I shall make it anyway. After all, no one can fire me since I am retired, and if worst comes to worst, I can eat my Hereford cows.

Before I touch the holy mountain, let me say that college-bound students should be taught enough about the catalog and reference tools to make it possible for them to do the research they will need to do in college. However, we should take a critical look at our plan to train all other high-school students. In 1965, the latest year for which there are complete statistics, 28 per cent of the high-school graduates of Baltimore went to college. In addition, 2.6 per cent enrolled for part-time courses. This 30.6 per cent of high-school graduates should have been taught the use of the catalog and reference tools. To the remaining 69.4 per cent we have done more harm than good by our insistence on teaching them how to use the catalog and tools of reference and research. The arguments against such instruction as I see them are:

*(a) It cannot be taught successfully.* The ALA Ad Hoc Committee on Instruction in the Use of Libraries says, "The great majority of students do not master library skills, and do not feel impelled to gain proficiency

in them." The committee, however, does not despair. They plan to "Hit 'em again harder" with new devices and more instruction. For many years the schools of the Baltimore-Washington metropolitan district have given tireless instruction in the use of the catalog and reference tools all through high school and to some extent in the lower grades. The surveyors working with Dr. Bundy looked for this trained patron who needed to do simple research, and where do you think they found him? At the shelves, looking through rows of books— hoping to wrest from them the information needed. The survey says, "He browses through the shelves hoping to find what he wants but is not likely to use reference books, library catalogs, or to seek help from a librarian. He is even less likely to make use of other library services and resources such as periodical indexes." If the survey is correct, how many hours, days, and years of instruction have failed to pay off! Methods of teaching this skill may change and improve, but however many variables we introduce, one constant remains—the student who does not wish to learn, and so, cannot be taught. Moreover, if the library world keeps abreast of the times, surely computers will eventually supply the material needed for school assignments. Meantime, the public library could make available instruction in the use of the catalog and reference tools for those who wish to learn. Attractive instructional devices such as those used by the National Geographic Society in Washington, D.C., might lead many patrons to wish to teach themselves the skills of research.

(b) *Our burning passion to force the adolescent to use the catalog has damaged our relations with him.* I have seen librarians demand that a youngster look up a book in the catalog when it was within arm's reach of the librarian. Probably the most hated six words in these United States of America are "Look it up in the catalog." Here is what some teenagers say in the survey: "In general, the librarians are fairly helpful as long as you never make the mistake of asking where a book is. Do this, and the librarian 'sweetly' says, 'What's the matter, don't you know how to use the catalog?' " Another: "I feel library service could be improved in that sometimes the librarians are too lazy to help you. Many times I have asked where a certain book is and she will say, 'Look it up in the catalog.' I feel this is not right. . . . Thank you for letting me express my opinion." One of the adult patrons spoke of librarians who, like some tradespeople, showed "the tyranny of petty authority," which, right or wrong, seems to be the idea in the heads of teenagers.

Further bound by our obsession, if a class from a neighborhood school comes for a visit to a branch library, we often entertain them royally with a lesson in the catalog when we might, instead, have interested them in Dostoevski's analysis of the criminal mind, A. B. Guthrie's depiction of the mountain man, or Van Gogh's passion to capture the essence of life in paint and color.

*(c) Our argument for teaching all students to use the catalog is based on a fallacy.* Library literature puts it this way: "The student should acquire proficiency in the independent use of library resources as an essential part of his formal education, and in support of his continuing self-education." We public librarians have honestly convinced ourselves that students now in high school will avidly continue their self-education throughout their adult lives, for which they will need to make continued use of the tools of research. The fact of the matter is that very few of these people will ever put foot inside the public library, and as was said above, half of those who do come want a good book to read rather than informational material. Most people live out their lives unaware of a need for books. No one ever inspired them to read for pleasure and they get along without looking up information. As for continued self-education, that is the last item on their agenda. I would guess that not one in a thousand citizens in any of our big cities is continuing his self-education to the extent of needing to know how to do research, and these we can continue to help or teach how to help themselves if they wish to know. Nor is it just the unread masses who fall short here. It is possible that librarians let a day slip now and then when they do not pursue "continuing self-education." A faculty member of a well-known university recently sent out a questionnaire to library administrators that contained a question on their professional reading and was surprised to find that few of them had read any books in their field in the last year or two.

*(d) If we gave up our futile attempt to teach everyone to use the catalog, the time saved could be spent in the intensive promotion of reading.* We could use the time for more class visits to talk about books, assembly programs on reading, book lists, reading clubs, and above all, work with individuals on the floor of the library. Even if we agreed that it is desirable for the 69.4 per cent who will not go to college to master the catalog and even if we succeeded in teaching all of them to do so, we would still have misused the time if instead we might have engendered in them a love of reading. The principles of education hold that the teaching of a skill has less value than the development of a cultural attitude.

*5. We are not meeting new challenges with new ideas.*

It is common knowledge that in the last twenty years the population of the American city has changed. In the past the public library catered to the well-heeled middle class to which most of us belonged. Today most of these people have fled the city, leaving behind the poor, the disadvantaged, the culturally deprived. Instead of college-bound, well-fed, well-mannered young people, we have thousands of adolescents who live in ghettos on relief, without a father and with a mother who never finished the third grade. In their homes these people are unlikely to hear what we think of as interesting conversation. There is little mention of good taste, little talk of ethical standards. Too many of them drop out of school, commit crimes, take dope, join mobs, and hate all authority and established institutions. The whole concept of voluntary reading is foreign to them. These conditions have made little difference in the public library's mode of procedure. The books are still on the shelves for those who wish to borrow them. This method, which never was too successful with the middle classes, is doomed to failure with the masses. Our new social crisis calls for new solutions.

An article entitled "Schools Make News" in the *Saturday Review* (May 21, 1966) began, "Pleasure books, books to read just for fun, are seldom seen, much less owned, by children and adults from disadvantaged areas. None lurk on shelves in their homes to be picked up and browsed through at off moments. Books are largely alien to their environment." The article went on to say that to counter this deprivation the Fund for the Advancement of Education had granted $200,000 to VISTA to equip them with portable paperback libraries suited to the needs of the people with whom they work.[7] I understand this project has not yet realized its full potential, but it seems the sort of undertaking in which the public library should be engaged.

Is it not possible that the solution of our problem may lie in going out to the people instead of waiting for them to come in to us?

Has not Dr. Fader's experiment with the delinquent boys of the Maxey School something to say to us? His *Hooked on Books* [1966] sounds like the beginning of a breakthrough.

There should be a regular national program on TV sponsored by ALA that would dramatize books and reading in such a highly professional, effective way that libraries all over the nation would feel its impact. Surely we could be as interesting as the family wash, bad breath, and tired blood.

Solutions for our problems could be found. But we need administrators concerned with the problem who have the ability to release talent. Then we need young-adult librarians dedicated to establishing rapport with the city kid and convincing him that the public library can furnish him not only with the informational material he needs, but also with the wonder and joy of reading. The book is our message.

Ho! every one that thirsteth, come ye to the waters,
and he that hath no money, come ye, buy and eat;
yea, come, buy wine and milk without money and without price.

[*Isaiah 55:1*]

# The Fair Garden
# and the Swarm of Beasts

In *The Old Librarian's Almanac* [1773] Jared Bean sets forth some guiding principles for his profession. Among them we read, "So far as your authority will permit it, exercise great Discrimination as to which Persons shall be admitted to the use of the Library. For the Treasure House of Literature is no more to be thrown open to the ravages of the unreasoning Mob, than is a Fair Garden to be laid unprotected at the Mercy of a Swarm of Beasts.

"Question each Applicant closely. See that he be a Person of good Reputation, scholarly Habits, sober and courteous Demeanor. Any mere Trifler, a Person that would Dally with Books, or seek in them shallow amusement, may be Dismissed without delay."

Jared Bean also has a message for those of us concerned with the teenager and the library: "No Person younger than twenty years (save if he be a Student, of more than eighteen years, and vouched for by his Tutor) is on any pretext to enter the Library. Be suspicious of Women. They are given to the Reading of frivolous Romances, and at all events, their presence in the Library adds little to (if it does not, indeed, detract from) that aspect of Gravity, Seriousness and Learning which is its greatest glory. . . ."

Dear Jared, hordes of young adults are pouring into our libraries, devouring the information in books. Indeed, the Treasure House of Literature has been thrown open to the ravages of the unreasoning mob and your fair garden lies "unprotected at the Mercy of a Swarm of Beasts."

Some have tried locking the teenagers out in the evenings; others have isolated them in certain rooms without access to the library as a whole; still others put up with them, crying inwardly and sometimes outwardly at the desecration. Young hands are reaching out for books and more books. Students are asking endlessly for help in finding

---

The above section was first published in *Library Journal*, September 1, 1965, 3379–83. *Ed.*

material for school assignments. Unhappy librarians say with some justification that adults are so dismayed by this invasion of youth that they do not make use of the library. If we could only get rid of these youngsters, our libraries would be more like Jared Bean's, the books protected from use, and unhappy librarians would find their problems solved. They wouldn't be librarians any more, for staffs could be cut from 50 to 75 per cent.

Certainly, there are many librarians with vision who are delighted to have the young people. They realize this invasion of young people could be quite meaningful for the future and wish they might serve teenagers better. But what is better? What is the best we might do for them?

These questions bring us to a serious consideration of the function of the public library as it serves youth. For the moment, suppose we had no problems of space, of book stock, of staff. If fairy godmothers and rich citizens and generous budget directors gave us carte blanche, how would we proceed? More than likely, we would purchase new encyclopedias, history reference books, everything we could find on the Elizabethan theatre in duplicate, more foreign language records, more about the UN. We might provide more individual study tables, more trained staff, more people who could take the daily grind. In other words, we would greatly enlarge our reference services. This would be wonderful; but would it be enough?

In this speeded-up civilization when people send in reservations for seats on the first moonflight and Mars has been on *Candid Camera*, big business and the institutions of society are reexamining their policies and procedures to see if they are adequate for the space age. I should like to propose this question for consideration by those concerned for the public library: If the library answers the inquiries it receives with courtesy and reasonable speed, if it provides a rich collection of books on all subjects for the reader to select from as he chooses, if it provides a staff able and willing to answer questions requiring research or knowledge of books, has it discharged its full duty to society? In other words, is the provision of a building, staff, and books enough, or is the public library in any way responsible for the fact that though we have one of the best library systems in the world, Americans read less than any other Western democratic people? That a very small percentage of the adults in most of our large cities are registered in the library and that a smaller percentage of those registered use their cards very often? According to polls taken, citizens of this country do not read on the average more than four books a year and many of those books are of a very poor quality indeed. Here are the nonfiction best sellers of 1963 as listed in *Publishers' Weekly*, in order of popularity:

*Happiness Is a Warm Puppy*
*Security Is a Thumb and a Blanket*
*J.F.K.: The Man and the Myth*
*Profiles in Courage*
*O Ye Jigs and Juleps!*
*Better Homes and Gardens Bread Cook Book*
*Pillsbury's Family Cook Book*
*I Owe Russia $1200*
*Heloise's Housekeeping Hints*
*Better Homes and Gardens Baby Book*[8]

While the many book clubs and the proliferation of paperbacks have stimulated reading, we cannot by any stretch of the imagination say that the citizens of the United States, who are expected to lead the free world, are reading enough to make them worthy of the trust. We can't derive much understanding and vision from cuddly children's books, cookbooks, and Bob Hope.

Perry of Harvard said, "The test of society is the quality of the persons who compose it."[9] Books can enrich the quality of the reader but informational books alone are not enough. Books that teach us are important but books that change us are wonderful. As a barefoot child on a Texas cotton farm, my first acquaintance with nobility came when my mother read to me the story of Ruth from the King James version of the Bible. Her "entreat me not to leave thee" expanded the horizons of my spirit as did David's lament for Absalom. When he cried in despair, "O Absalom, my son, my son, would God that I had died for thee," I wept with him. In my later years I have become a bigger person since my vigil on the mountaintop with Kumalo the night his son was executed in *Cry, the Beloved Country.* Agnes Keith set me thinking of the wonder of being able to identify with the other person whoever he is and wherever he lives.[10] She established perfect rapport with the natives of Borneo, the sophisticated guests she entertained, with the sad little Filipino boy singing in his shabby slum, even with the Japanese who imprisoned and tortured her. Baroness Blixen's *Out of Africa* [1964] gave me a new perspective on the African—not as a savage or a pathetic primitive but as a remarkable man with a different heritage. From her first sentence, "I had a farm in Africa at the foot of the Ngong Hills . . . " I felt I was in the company of a sophisticated, wise, humorous woman who saw life more clearly than I. *The Education of Hyman Kaplan* and *Life with Father* showed me how much richer humor is if it has an undercurrent of sympathy or poignancy.[11] From James Baldwin I have learned the deep suffering prejudice inflicts on the intelligent, sensitive Negro.

When I read Saint-Exupéry's *Wind, Sand and Stars* [1939], I found expressed the philosophy I had begun to feel but had never formulated for myself. His long, lyrical definition of man ends with, "To be a man is to feel that in setting one's stone, one is contributing to the building of the world." Alfred North Whitehead in his *Aims of Education* [1957] summed up what I have been attempting to say when he wrote, "Culture is activity of thought, and receptiveness to beauty and humane feeling. Scraps of information have nothing to do with it. A merely well-informed man is the most useless bore on God's earth. . . ."

I am grateful for my schooling, and the facts I learned were important and necessary, but I would be poor indeed if my reading had stopped with my schooling—and that is exactly what does happen to most high-school and college graduates. In a Gallup poll taken a few years ago, it was reported that half of our high-school graduates and a fourth of our college graduates had not read a single book in that year. The Deiches survey recently made states that Baltimore high-school students read while in school to complete assignments, better their grades, or please their teachers, and that when their schooling ends, all too often, so does their reading.[12]

Reading for understanding and enrichment has always been important, but today it is urgent. John Ciardi says modern man is really Neanderthal man with a push button. Someone else has said he is the old barbarian with vast new instruments to use. We must make Neanderthal man into a citizen of the modern world very quickly before be blows himself to smithereens; the old barbarian must become a gentleman fast, before he swings his club. All social institutions must work to this end, but libraries have a heavy responsibility, for it is within the covers of books that man may find the ideas and understanding that will civilize him.

Just making books available is not enough, just helping with school assignments is not enough. Neanderthal man must look on books as more than the tools of formal education. He must taste the flavor of rich, unrequired reading, as Lamb's character tasted the flavor of roast pig and found that it was good.[13] The best time to persuade the barbarian to read is when he is young, for this is when he is most receptive to ideas and most responsive to them.

Dora Smith, a distinguished reading specialist in the National Council of Teachers of English, discussing high-school and college reading, wrote, "Left to themselves, young people tend to read within a narrow area and in materials which afford them little real challenge. They need the guidance of sympathetic and widely read adults in identifying, extending and intensifying their interests. Many of them have problems which they could solve if they were but aware of them. Others have latent interests which need only to be challenged. Still others know specifically what their interests are but are unaware of materials available for pursuing them."

Not everyone can persuade the young barbarian to undertake the voluntary reading of books. And here is where the special librarian for the young adult enters the picture. To work successfully with young adults he must understand and like teenagers and be able to establish a rapport with them based on mutual respect and liking. He must be a genuine person with a sense of humor and emotional balance, outgoing rather than self-centered. Above all, he must know books—hundreds of them—on a wide range of subjects and on various reading levels. He must know how to make books seem interesting and important to all readers, from the most deprived to the most fortunate and accelerated. He must be able to discuss books after they are read and constantly enrich and enlarge the quality of reading done. Just waiting on people pleasantly is failing them. He must develop readers to their full potential.

Someone has said, "Paradoxically, as the world grows smaller, men must grow larger." If we sit tight in our chairs when young people come into the library, pointing to the catalog, answering questions when asked, encouraging teenagers to browse around and find a book but never approaching them or making suggestions for voluntary reading, we are doing very little to ensure that they will grow larger. We fail the boy who finds Erle Stanley Gardner and plans to spend the winter reading all his mysteries if we do not interest him in *All Quiet on the Western Front,* people of other countries, or such books as Horgan's *Distant Trumpet* [1960] and Braithwaite's *To Sir, with Love* [1959]. Nor can we allow meaningful, moving books to sit on the shelves indefinitely because their titles do not attract casual browsers. The young-adult librarian must be an artist. He must have the original passion or capacity for feeling that any artist has. Then, he must learn how to perform—the technique to make his work effective.

The young-adult librarian must be creative. He must devise ways to sell the idea of reading for reading's sake not only to individuals but to groups. He must make of himself an effective speaker and visit schools to talk to classes informally of books to read for pleasure. He must learn to dress windows and make displays of books to catch the eye. He must think constantly of new ways to advertise the world's best product.

To be a successful young-adult librarian takes some doing. It calls for fertilization of the mind, enlargement of the spirit, identification with the community, constant reading, dedication, and old-fashioned hard work. But all these qualities are not enough without a sympathetic administration. In these days when libraries are besieged by Jared

Bean's "unreasoning Mob," when there is not standing room in the reference department, when the staff is literally inundated with requests for materials for school assignments, it seems to many administrators a kind of extravagant luxury to assign one of their most gifted librarians to hand out books for pleasure and to talk to young people about books when everyone else is working at fever heat to find the height of Mount Blanc, the structure of the frog, a picture of the uniform worn in the U.S. army in 1812. How can the administrator justify a staff member's taking full time to talk to a young reader about the underlying philosophy of *1984*, Golding's concept of man's nature, or what Griffin learned about prejudice when he lived his *Black Like Me*?[14] To some administrators, this is not as urgent as answering questions related to school assignments. Maybe it isn't so urgent but it might be more important. The public library must be more than the handmaiden of the schools.

So far we have discussed our cultivation of what Jared Bean called "the Fair Garden," suggesting better seed and more fertilization, with emphasis on more effective layout. Let us now look at an adjoining patch of weeds. There are 38 million people in this country who live in poverty. Many are unemployed, living on relief to the third and fourth generation—slum dwellers and dropouts who are more than problems. They threaten our economy and constitute one of the gravest dangers to our security. Unless they are reeducated, retrained, absorbed into the labor market, and taught how to live, there is trouble ahead. The government realizes the seriousness of the problem. More than that, the schools are reconsidering the kind of education that has failed these people. It is essential, it seems to me, for the library to revise its middle-class approach and devise new ways of making books a part of the lives of these people who desperately need the ideas found in books. We must study to find books that speak the language of young people from fatherless families where the mother didn't finish the fourth grade, where no one reads or discusses ethics, where work is a strange concept, where only the relief check is real. For young people from such backgrounds the simple teenage romance or baseball story scorned by literary critics may have a great deal to say about wholesome family life, sportsmanship, codes of honor, good manners, and so forth. If we have no suitable books, we should find out just what we need and get publishers to produce them.

Then we should master the technique of introducing these people to reading and study to lead them eventually from simple books about the world they understand to books that will interpret to them the world they never knew. James Baldwin was one of these people who, as a despairing child of the Harlem slums, went to the library in his neighborhood and systematically read every book in it in a desperate search for identity with people outside the wretched world he knew. He found it when he read the great books and discovered he was bound to other men in suffering. Too few of these young people come to the library of their own accord, but we must not abandon them.

We must not be content to work only with people who happen to come to the library, excusing ourselves by saying it is hopeless to make readers of most people when often it is ourselves and our methods that are at fault. For too long we have waited on young people rather than developing their highest reading potential. For too long we have been satisfied to furnish information only, when enriching books were standing on the shelves.

In an annual report of the Toledo Public Library I read, "Man is not the only animal that talks. Monkeys chatter and signal to each other, crows caw, bees direct each other to new sources of nectar by intricate dances. But man is the only animal who can talk from one century or millennium to another. And he does it through books and libraries." Our assignment is to make sure that when mankind tells the story of his struggle to the light, of his suffering, his failures, his joy and love and faith—that the message gets through to the people here and now.

## Let the Beasts In

With all its machinery for charging out books, organizing, preserving, and dispensing information, with all its technicians trained to operate the machinery, the public library is as new as tomorrow. As for professional services to the individual and the community, however, the library is becoming an anachronism. Never effective in dealing with the nation's reading problems, the library is slipping further and further behind the times.

In most school libraries the promotion of reading is a lost art. Many school librarians do not go beyond doing reference work, supplementing the curriculum, and teaching the use of the catalog and reference tools. As a librarian attached to a state department of public instruction put it, "Many schools have felt a need to indicate the change in the image and role of the school library by changing the name of the area to Media Center, Instructional Materials Center, Resource Center, etc." Whatever happened to the book and the pleasure of reading it? Hey, miss, where is the library?

In the past, middle-aged people were in the majority. It was the well-to-do, established, conservative "pillars of society" who called the tune. In this new era, it is the young people who are in the majority. They are alive, concerned about society, active in politics, intolerant of sham and hypocrisy. They look at society's institutions with critical eyes and force establishments to offer proof of things previously accepted without question.

Industry and the professions are becoming increasingly aware of the importance of youth. *The New York Times* says Macy's now aims its advertising at the twenty-five-year-olds. The movie industry has found that over half its patrons are under thirty and they have had something to think about since *The Graduate*. This unheralded, inexpensive picture had something to say and spoke to youth in youth's language. As a result, waiting lines formed for blocks down the streets of cities and towns all over the nation and many young people went to see it five or six times. The reaction of young people will have a marked effect from here on as far as the motion picture industry is concerned.

Lawyers are beginning to say that they must cease to rely so heavily on decisions made in the past for this is a new age with new problems. High schools are seeking to interest more young people in finishing their educations and colleges are reexamining their philosophy and curricula to gain the confidence of young people. Ministers and priests often join with youth to protest injustice, and the Catholic mass has been set to the music of young people.

In the face of all this the public library, like the Southerner waving a Confederate flag, lives in its past and continues to center its planning around the solid, middle-aged citizen. It resents the fact that high-school students fill up the chairs and wear out the books in the reference room, hoping the day will soon come when the students will disappear to be confined more and more to the school library. Public librarians consider young people an interruption to business, yet they *are* the business, more so than the middle-aged adults the librarians are waiting for.

We know that young people make the heaviest use of our reference services, and evidence points to their being the majority of our readers as well. In a recent Gallup poll, it was found that 58 per cent of the sample of 1,510 American adults said they had "never read a book from cover to cover," 11 per cent said they had read a book during the last eleven months, and 5 per cent said they remembered reading a book more than a year before, not since. But the poll found that far more young adults (in their twenties) had read a book than older adults. Evidently there is a correlation between age and reading books.

Yet the public library puts its emphasis on adult services, making young-adult work subsidiary. It purchases its books and arranges its services primarily for adults, allowing young people to make use of its books and services if they must but without attempting to make them feel welcome, without, with a few exceptions, making special provisions for them, and without delegating a well-read, friendly staff member to make books meaningful and to share with them the joy of reading. As a profession, the public library is "stuck fast in yesterday," still protecting the fair garden from the swarm of beasts. It is time to let them in.

# ⚚ VII ⚚

# I Once Did See
# Joe Wheeler Plain

On July 1, 1926, young Joseph Wheeler arrived in Baltimore as the head librarian of the Enoch Pratt Free Library, probably the worst public library in any large city in the U.S.A. It was housed in a gloomy old Victorian dwelling on Mulberry Street with an overflow in three private dwellings around the corner on Cathedral Street and a patchwork of branches. The staff was made up mostly of genteel women of fairly advanced years who suddenly became librarians when Enoch Pratt endowed the library and offered his friends' daughters a chance to make pin money in a ladylike way. In the entire system, there was not one trained librarian and only five college graduates.

Though all the books were out of sight in the stacks, the oldest ones were in a dark basement along with mice and rats, which, the timid "slip chasers" avoided by writing "out" on the call slips and themselves remaining on the floor above. Only two books—one fiction and one nonfiction—could be withdrawn at a time. My husband, who was a patron as a boy, said the borrower was given two "asks." If a book came up but was not what he wanted, he had to take it anyway for he had asked for it, hadn't he? If neither of the two came up, he went home as he had had his "asks." Kate Coplan remembers that on the counter

---

This chapter was presented as a paper at the American Library History Round Table in Dallas, Texas, June 1971, under the program title "How Firm a Foundation: A Tribute to Joseph L. Wheeler." It was added in the 1974 edition of this work. *Ed.*

of the room known as the "delivery room" stood a small glass case holding about two hundred books. The reader could point to a book he wanted to take home in addition to the two borrowed. If, on examination, the reader decided he did not want the book, he could choose another but no third choice was allowed if the second were declined.

When Joe Wheeler arrived, he put seven thousand of the best books on open shelves. He brought in two trained librarians, one to head childrens' work and one adult work. The book collection was weeded, reorganized, and expanded. He radiated energy, cheerfulness, and enthusiasm for the job. He was everywhere, encouraging, showing appreciation of work well done, and enlisting ideas from the staff. News stories about the changes appeared and Baltimore, which previously had had little regard for or interest in the library, began to sit up and take notice. Before long Pratt's circulation had increased 113 per cent. When Joe Wheeler pointed this out to the municipal authorities in an attempt to obtain a large appropriation, one of the officials asked, "Who the hell told you to increase the circulation 113 per cent?"

Meantime, the trustees were not helping. Enoch Pratt had appointed a self-perpetuating board of upper-class gentlemen of fine old Maryland families who worried over this brash young librarian. For one thing, the band around his straw hat was too loud and they felt obliged to tell him so. But they were worried even more by his irritating insistence that they should provide the city with a new library building. He brought the matter up at every meeting, and each time they told him it was "being considered" until they could stand it no longer; then they told him not to bring the matter up again, that it was closed.

He simply had to have that building and could not let go. He went to the mayor and found there was a remote chance that the legislature would pass an enabling act allowing funds for the building the very next day, the last of the session, but only if pressure was brought to bear. Dr. Wheeler figured his only hope lay in enlisting the aid of the one board member who seemed sympathetic, a prominent surgeon. He rushed to the Hopkins hospital, found the surgeon in his underwear preparing for an operation, and started talking. The surgeon said he would think it over while he operated, decided to help, rode with Dr. Wheeler to Annapolis at the crack of dawn the next day, and got the money.

Dr. Wheeler had his own ideas about that building. It was not to be located in a quiet suburb approached by a winding, tree-bordered drive. It was not to have a lot of steps or a marble enclosed vestibule. He wanted the building in the very heart of the city, where the people were—on the street level so women could wheel their baby buggies into it. There would be show windows across the front, and the first thing the patron would see would be books, thousands of them out in view—everywhere—and there would be color and light and beauty all around. In this building, businessmen and others who approached the service desks would be waited on by smiling, efficient, pretty girls. He used to stand in the central hall and smile and look at them. It did him good to see them at the desks, just as Samuel Pepys said it did him good to see Nell Gwynn's underwear hanging on the clothesline. It did the city's businessmen good too.

When the library got settled in the new building, he brought a secondhand printing press and hired an inexpensive, tobacco-chewing printer to run it. He composed broadsides of brief biographies of great men who achieved success through reading and persuaded a laundry to put them on cards inserted into freshly laundered shirts. He had a dairy delivering lists with the milk and seed merchants distributing lists of books on flower and vegetable gardening with seed purchases. In 1929, Baltimore's anniversary year, at one of the largest department stores two pretty girls in colonial costume with baskets filled with library book lists stood at the store's main entrance handing out leaflets to all. When he heard a live tarantula had been found down at the docks in a cargo of bananas, he got the tarantula and featured it in a display of books on spiders.

But his greatest achievement in the beginning was the creation of a truly professional staff, starting from scratch. He had an uncanny knack of sizing up people and in his quiet, friendly way, making them experts. He set up a training class for promising young applicants where the students were given basic courses in working with children and adults, understanding the catalog, doing reference work, and becoming acquainted with a wide range of books. On his frequent rounds about the library, he watched among the patrons for young people with the personality and potentiality he needed for members of the staff. One of the department heads told of the time her attractive cousin came to take her to dinner. As they left, the girl said, "While I was waiting for you, a man came up to me and asked me if I would like to work in the library. I told him no, that being around all those books was like being in a morgue." What a blow that remark must have been, for it was his anxiety to make the library a beautiful, joyous place that had led him to ask her if she would like to work there.

Soon after he arrived at the Pratt Library, he looked over his untrained staff to see who had possibilities. For one thing, he had a secretary who had no college training; but she was so vibrant, charming, and efficient, he decided she did not belong behind the scenes but should be shared with the public. He transferred her to the Circulation Department, from which she advanced to a branch librarianship and, eventually, to head the branch system.

Kate Coplan was a young assistant replacing old, dirty, wornout books in the order department. She had no college training; but because she was eager and had ideas, he decided to see if he could teach her to handle publicity. She had no idea of public relations but he lent her his *Library and the Community* with his philosophy of making the library and its resources as useful as possible to every segment of the city and to every individual—a cradle-to-grave service. Before the new building came into being, he sent her into the heart of Baltimore's business district to borrow vacant store windows. The library had no truck, but Kate had the part-time assistance of a seventy-three-year-old janitor who carried the basket of books in one hand and a pail and cleaning equipment in the other. After borrowing a bucket of water from a corner drug store, they would wash the window to be used and set up the display. Kate says Dr. Wheeler taught her how to plan displays, write news releases, and compile booklists. With his encouragement and guidance, she became nationally known in the field of public relations, won the friendship of the city's newsmen, and was frequently offered positions with commercial firms.

As for me—in 1932 I entered the training class by God's grace and because of Joe Wheeler's gambling instincts. I had just been fired from the teaching profession and was under a cloud, to put it mildly. As he could not resist the impulse to see if he could make a silk purse out of a sow's ear, he agreed to let me enter the training class. When I taught school, the supervisors who paid surprise visits always looked first at my window shades, no two of which were ever at the same level. Then they looked at the thermostat, which was either too high or too low. Dr. Wheeler never told my library supervisor of my dark past. He never checked on me but assumed I was intelligent and well meaning. He encouraged me to be creative and to discuss my ideas with him even if they seemed far out. He let me try doubtful schemes and never reproved me by word or look if I came a cropper. When I asked him if I might drive a horse-drawn book wagon in the slums in the summertime, he said, "I don't think it will work, but you can try it." I was drunk with his confidence and worked my head off. We all worked, but so did he.

Soon after I was put in charge of the young adult collection at Central, I edited a vacation reading list with what seemed to me a very clever design for the cover. A few months after it was distributed, my supervisor showed me a crude copy of the design on a list some little library in another state had used without asking permission. I was furious. I took the list to Dr. Wheeler in his office and laid it on his desk in high dudgeon. He looked at it and smiled and said, "Well?"

I replied with some heat. "They copied my list and did not even ask my permission!"

"I don't understand why you are mad," he said. "Isn't your aim in life to get teenagers to read books?"

"Yes," I replied.

"Well, if you have an idea that works, aren't you glad for it to be used anywhere it will help?" After working under Joseph Wheeler for a while, one could say with the Psalmist, "I will lift up mine eyes [Psalm 121:1]."

I never saw him leave the library for the day without books under his arm. Books excited him and he was daily in the order department laying his hands reverently on the new books, for any one of them, he often said, might change the plans and life of whoever read it. I remember when a prison requested a list of books for its library, I was assigned the compilation of the list because in my work with young adults, I was supposed to be familiar with readable books in various fields. Along with the request had come a listing of the prisoners' many interests and as most of them fell in fields with which I was unfamiliar, I leaned heavily on the department heads. I added what little I knew and took the pack of some five hundred slips to Dr. Wheeler. I sat open-mouthed as he went through the slips, commenting on almost every title with such remarks as: "There is a better book on orchards by Jameson." "There is a later edition of this book." "Try the government pamphlet instead of this book." "This is newer, but Floyd is better."

He was obsessed with service to the individual and kept an idea list on his desk of ways to serve the city better. He spoke of the great pleasure he felt in watching people, each with his individual background, lined up at the loan desk—each getting the same attention, regardless. He defined librarianship as the fascinating profession of helping all kinds of people get the information, ideas, convictions, and encouragement they seek in every aspect of their lives. A few weeks before he died, an interview with him was recorded on tapes, to which I have been allowed to listen. There were long pauses and extraneous reminiscences, for death was staring him in the face and it was difficult to concentrate. After one long pause, he called out clearly, "Service! Service is a wonderful word." Later he said, "Censorship, automation, regionalization, and such are today the concerns of the staff while the poor customer stands on one foot on the other side of the desk and who cares about him?" He saw to it that every person who entered the door of the Pratt Library was given the best possible service with courtesy and grace.

I remember there was on the staff a brilliant girl with a marvelous book background who was unsurpassed at her best; but at her worst, she could be rude. One day when she was at her worst, an old lady fell into her hands in the fiction department and was given the works, at which she went to Dr. Wheeler's office and reported the matter. He sent for the assistant who returned thoroughly chastened. She told me confidentially,

"He made me feel like a fool. I was expecting to be bawled out but he was calm and looked sad. He said, 'Lucy, you know that old Mrs. Jenkins you waited on this afternoon? Poor old thing. She walked clear across town with her feet hurting saying to herself that if she could just make it to the Pratt Library, she would get help and when she got here, you hurt her!' By the time he was through, I thought I would die."

"Listen," she continued, "If you ever see me starting to be mean to anybody ever again, for God's sake, stop me!"

He not only worked to make the Pratt Library effective. He wanted all the libraries of the nation to be effective. He encouraged Mary Barton to compile the booklet *A Guide to Reference Books* when she was head of the Reference Department. It is now in its sixth edition with Marion Bell as coeditor of the last edition; 80,000 copies have been distributed. Virginia Kirkus has often spoken of what his encouragement meant when she was hesitating to launch her project of prepublication book reviewing. Father Kortendick, head of the Catholic University Library School, told me of running into Dr. Wheeler at an ALA conference and the lift he got from Dr. Wheeler's praise of two of his projects. These are only a few examples of his ranging librarianship.

But back to the Pratt Library. St. Exupèry said, "A rock pile ceases to be a rock pile the moment a man of vision contemplates it, bearing within himself the image of a cathedral." And so, in ten years, this man of vision changed one of the worst urban libraries in America to one of the best in the world. He said once that in those years, he often felt a giant had him by the hand running with him so fast his own feet touched the ground about every five or six steps. He might have added that in this wild dash, he had his staff by the hand, and their feet, too, just touched the high spots. Despite the pressure, librarians often came to Pratt at a reduction in salary for the opportunity to train under him. It is remarkable how many who worked under his supervision became leaders in the profession. Among them are: Emerson Greenaway, Harold L. Hamill, Harold V. Tucker, Francis St. John, John Humphrey, Paul Howard, Joseph Shipman, Richard Sealock, Lillian Bradshaw, Stewart Sherman, Thurston Taylor, Amy Winslow, and many others. What public library is training such administrators today? Where is there available inservice training for librarians with potentialities? I was told recently that eight city libraries are searching for directors and even with the great surplus of librarians now available, the eight cities cannot find administrators with a vision of service who are book lovers, innovators, dedicated people who can excite a staff and through them, a whole community with books and the ideas they contain.[1]

But of all Dr. Wheeler's qualities, to me, the most inspiring was his concern for youth. When I took the entrance exam for the training class, one of the questions was, "If you were waiting on a young person and a U.S. senator came to your desk, what would you do?" Had I answered that I would let the child wait while I attended to the senator, it would probably have been curtains for me. One of the first things he did as the new librarian at Pratt was to change the borrowing privileges of children so that a child could always have one adult book if he wanted it. He told me he did this to protect children from those old maid librarians who did not realize the potentialities of some children.

Because there was no doubt in his mind of the power of the book and because he was challenged by the tremendous potential in youth, he felt there was no more important function of the public library than to cultivate and promote the voluntary reading of teenagers. In his last interview he said YA work was so horribly important, for at this time in their lives, young people must learn to love books; it would be tragic if they did not. He put some of the best read and most creative people on his staff on the floor of Central and the branches to win the confidence of teenagers and sell them the idea of rich voluntary reading. These librarians talked to classes in the schools, put on TV and radio programs, spoke to parents and teachers, and constantly devised ways of enriching teenagers with books.

He felt administrators of public libraries did not understand the importance of young adult work, did not see how obvious was the need for it. In his last days, he kept writing me that something was going on in New York state that bothered him. "There is a report," he wrote, "that is all wrong." For the public library to wash its hands of young people was to him unthinkable.

The public library's departure from Dr. Wheeler's conception of the importance of work with young adults could be the death knell of an institution fast losing vitality. There has always been hostility to teenagers in public libraries over the nation. Insecure librarians have always wanted to be identified with adults, not youth. They have kidded themselves into believing that if it were not for young people, captains of industry, industrialists, union leaders, directors of theaters, editors of newspapers would swarm into the library. We serve the bulk of our clientele, people under twenty-five, only as much as we must and are even considering making the public library off bounds to them. If we implement the report of the New York committee and the adults do not swarm in, we shall have committed suicide.

We have been frightened for years of the little old lady in tennis shoes, realizing our public image was too close to hers to be comfortable. In an effort to disprove any association with her, we have embraced every new advance in technology—the computer, charging machines, teletype, AV. We have done every new thing possible but have neglected the book and the individual. Along this line, W. H. Webb of the College and Reference Library section of the Canadian Library Association wrote recently, "Just as the 'little old librarian' of recent memory was written off because she could neither comprehend nor accept computer manipulation of library problems, so the 'modern academic librarian' is in imminent peril of being ignored by the new spirit on the campus. The new spirit does not demand ever larger libraries, ever larger and larger computers. . . . Rather, the new spirit suggests that the purpose of the librarian is to help explain, with all the tools available, mankind to man and each man to himself. If the library and its librarians fend off the questioners and avoid confrontation with the new consciousness, then surely they will lose the opportunity of coming close to the concerns of present day students. They will not touch reality and they will surely be forgotten."[2]

I hear that some of the young librarians of this sonic age of Aquarius consider Wheeler old hat—no computer, no AV, too much emphasis on books. Nor was he impressed with them. He called them McLuhanatics. So far, these McLuhanatics who allow technological gadgets to take precedence over the book and reading have not shaken up present day society or even one city as Dr. Wheeler shook up Baltimore by the simple but more difficult procedure of persuading people to read books. We are withering on the vine with our failure to produce leaders and with young librarians becoming disillusioned with the profession. A return to Joseph L. Wheeler's philosophy might save us. That is, if we had faith in the book, read it as he did, believed in youth, and turned heaven and earth to put books into the hands of people. If we got out on the streets, if we won the hearts of the young and made an impact on the masses, we might hold our young assistants and develop leaders to renew us in the future. Whatever methods we are using today are not effective enough. Possibly if we followed the trails Dr. Wheeler blazed, we might convince the people of this country that libraries and the nourishment of the mind are as essential as physical necessities. If we do not, we may be reduced to a few little old ladies in tennis shoes stuffing computers; for in the future there will be more and more people and less and less money and idealistic young taxpayers of tomorrow will probably not support us when the masses of people are hungry, ill clothed, and imprisoned in ghettos.

Joseph L. Wheeler, the activist, not only set the city of Baltimore afire with books as bombs, but he revolutionized librarianship over the nation in the almost two hundred administrative and building projects for which he was consultant as well as by his writings on buildings and the relationship of the library to the community. Among his more important books is *The Practical Administration of Public Libraries* written with Herber Goldhor. In order to keep the price of the book down to $7.50 so that even small libraries could afford it, he volunteered to accept only minimal royalties.

This man was also a "character." His daughter, Mary, wrote me that he loved to drive a car and could not resist speeding. He had a lot of trouble with cops over stop signs. When Mary was a little girl, in the days when cops could collect fines, he was arrested for running through a stop sign. The cop demanded a fine and Dr. Wheeler told him he did not have in hand the fee demanded. "All right," the cop said. "It's jail for you." Mary cried so loud and hard, the cop let him off. "As we drove away," Mary wrote, "guess what he pulled out from between the cushions?" You see, he didn't actually have it *in hand*. When he was eighty-two, he drove from New Hampshire to Wisconsin and was clocked going one hundred miles per hour for ten miles. He reported that he and the policeman had a nice visit and he was let off with a warning.

Tact was not his strong point. When he saw other librarians mismanaging libraries, he sometimes gave them free, unsolicited, and unappreciated advice. When he was consultant for the Dallas Public Library many years ago, he told them they should get rid of some dead wood and put Lillian Bradshaw in charge. She was fairly new at the library and a low man on the totem pole at the time. The remark did her no good with the staff and she had to talk fast to keep in their good graces. While his suggestion was not tactful, the idea was not so bad—just a bit ahead of time as were his other ideas. When the city fathers denied him funds and his board would not help, he blew his top. His daughter says he would have been in one controversy after another if her mother had not forced him to "keep his cool." In his eighty-sixth year, he plunged into the fight over aid to parochial schools by writing red-hot letters to the local paper. On his deathbed, when Mary told him the hospital had put on his tray a dish of spinach which he despised, all he said was, "Hell!" And of course he willed his eyes to the eye bank. It is interesting to speculate on why he was never made president of ALA. Did he give some person in authority unsolicited advice? Was the establishment afraid he would rock the boat? At eighty-five, when Castleton State College in Vermont was without a librarian, he stepped in to fill the job until a librarian could be found. Then, he became head of the college's reference department under the same circumstances. Three of his sons became PhD's and John won the Fermi award in 1968.

I should like to close with a brief account of his last days gleaned from the diary he kept in 1970 when he was eighty-six. That year he achieved one of his heart's desires, something he had worked for long and hard—a grant of over $34,000 to the American Association for State and Local History for the preparation and publication of a manual on the collecting, handling, and servicing of local history materials in public and college libraries and here is the clincher—to be carried out over a twenty-eight month period by Joseph L. Wheeler with a committee to assist.

Though his strength was failing and he was having painful circulation problems, he spoke at ALA in Detroit to over seven hundred people on cataloging-in-source, another of his special interests. Fearful he might not have the strength to complete the reading of his paper, he asked Emerson Greenaway to stand by and take over if he failed but, he wrote in his diary, "I was able to finish by slowing down and a few waits."

The problem of circulation became more and more acute and he was in and out of the hospital; yet he kept up a flourishing correspondence about library matters, sometimes writing ten letters a day, such as one to a librarian in the South: "Why don't you write to the Superintendent of Documents about a half dozen indexes by major subject field of the detailed contents of the U.S. documents, organized just like the Wilson subject indexes? I realize this should go through some ALA committee but am so discouraged about the time it takes to get *anything* underway through ALA committees." He suggested to others that reading lists on U.S. history be prepared. And who could fail to be moved by his asking the Pratt Library in these times of frustration and despair to publish a reading list he called "Lift Up Your Hearts"?

July 30th, he wrote in the diary: "I wrote some letters. Very wobbly and weak today." August 19: "Pretty tired and foot ached." August 21: "Working on Building Manuscript." October 24: "I mailed 20 letters yesterday, not including letters to second hand booksellers." And again, "Working on Building Manuscript."

As Browning said:

> That low man seeks a little thing to do,
> Sees it and does it;
> This high man, with a great thing to pursue,
> Dies ere he know it.
>
> [from "A Grammarian's Funeral," 1855]

When he resigned from the Pratt Library, the *Baltimore Evening Sun* said in an editorial: "It is customary nowadays to speak of 'library science'! Ah, but the administration of a great library is still an art rather than a science. If there were in fact any such thing as library science, the impending resignation of Dr. Wheeler would be a matter of little moment, just install a new library scientist and let the wheels continue to turn. But since public library administration is an art, indeed one of the great arts, thousands of people in Baltimore will be wanting to know whether an artist of comparable stature is to succeed Dr. Wheeler."

In *Wind, Sand, and Stars*, St. Exupéry tells of an old gardener who lay dying. Thinking back on his lifetime of working with the earth and growing things, he called out, "And who will prune my trees for me when I am gone?" St. Exupéry extols him as a great soul "for he was bound by ties of love to all cultivable land and to all the trees of the world." So, Dr. Wheeler was bound by ties of love to all the books in libraries and to all the people who might read them. And who will prune his trees for him when he is gone?

# ❧ VIII ❧

# We Have Been True to You, Melvil Dewey, after Our Fashion

Where did the trouble start? With Melvil Dewey. All professions tend to glorify their founders and to hand down to succeeding generations principles and traditions that have gathered around them. There is Hippocrates, the Greek physician who is known as the father of medicine; Socrates, the great teacher; St. Augustine, a man of God; Cicero, the lawyer; and Melvil Dewey, the librarian and founder of the American Library Association.

Melvil Dewey was a genius who made a great contribution to libraries of the world when he showed us how to catalog, classify, and arrange printed matter so that information in books would be in order on the shelves and available to all. It seems ungrateful to ask for more but I believe we might not be in trouble today if this ingenious man had not stopped with organizing knowledge but had been equally concerned with getting the ideas and the culture in books into the minds of the people.

I doubt that Melvil Dewey was worried about the cultural poverty of the masses of people, for among his many activities he founded the Lake Placid Club and helped set up its charter, barring entrance to all Negroes, Jews, and tuberculars. As a result, when the New York Library Association a year or so ago decided to honor our founder and hold their annual meeting at his shrine, the Lake Placid Club, they had

---

This chapter was added in the 1974 edition. *Ed.*

101

to abandon the idea, for many librarians were Jewish, many were black, and those living in New York City were probably tubercular.

Dewey and the cofounders of ALA did not put great emphasis on the promotion of reading nor have many of their successors. Indeed, it is difficult to find in library literature where reading for any other reason than to find information is stressed. From the date of the establishment of the profession, a library has been thought of as a suitably housed collection of books and materials classified and organized by subject, indexed in a catalog, and administered by a staff trained in research who could be consulted if necessary and who checked the books in and out. This conception has come down almost intact to this day and has been developed into a highly efficient system that has afforded citizens of all ages and classes a free, reliable source of information for practically every need. This is, of course, a great boon to American society. And yet, ever since libraries were founded, the general public has cherished the idea that one goes to the library for a "good" book, meaning a book to enjoy. This idea still prevails, for a survey made by the University of Maryland library school found that half the patrons of the Baltimore-Washington Metropolitan District came to the library simply for a "good" book to read.

The book has been beloved over the world down through the ages as a symbol of wisdom and enrichment. People attribute to the printed word a kind of magic so potent that they throw what seem to them evil books into the fire to break their spells. For the reader, the book is escape when the world crowds in; it is courage and inspiration and vision; it is an extension and enrichment of one's limited experience. It is loved for these reasons rather than for the information it contains. We value the dictionary, the history of art, the scientific treatise, but we love with a burning passion *Romeo and Juliet*, Homer's *Odyssey*, and *Anna Karenina*.

As long as there have been libraries, people have thought of librarians as book lovers and have hoped if they walked into a library that they would find professionals who would introduce them to congenial and inspiring authors and share with them the joy of reading. Librarians in general have played along with this idealized image of the library and librarians. And they have taken to themselves status in the community as the book's ambassadors when, in fact, most of them do very little reading and are in reality technicians who know the mechanical processes of making books and the information in them available but are no more concerned for enlarging the vision of the masses than was Melvil Dewey.

The librarian is not so in love with what is inside books as the system under which they are organized. Above all else, he loves the catalog. He is obsessed with it and wants everybody in the United States to share with him the joy of mastering it. If we were half as excited about good reading, we could save the nation. When the school or public librarian speaks to a class of youngsters, he usually chooses the catalog and its workings as his subject. The students may not wish to hear about it but he tells them anyway. But the real fun comes when the youngster comes to the library and asks for help. That's when we really have the teenager over a barrel. The procedure is to smile sweetly and say, "Look it up in the catalog." Though our social life is meager and love may have passed us by, we still have the power to make the youngster pull out a drawer, write down a number, and then try to find the book on the shelf.

Though manipulating the system to retrieve information is our main concern, we do include in the book collection fiction and belles-lettres—but we play them down. We are careful in our circulation reports to list fiction and nonfiction separately so we can prove to the city fathers and everyone else, including other librarians, that we are doing serious business and are not encouraging people to waste time reading stories. It seems more professional to put up a display entitled "Know Your State!" rather than "History with a Novel Twist" or "Profiles in Courage," which would combine fiction and nonfiction.

We feel as modern as tomorrow because we have added to the system all the newest technological gadgets: microfilm, teletype, computers, cassettes, films, and so forth, but we still do not know what is inside the books nor how to make them meaningful to readers. We are more concerned for the system than for people and their pressing problems. Our books could throw light on the serious and portentous social problems of the nation if they were read, but we do not bestir ourselves to read them, much less persuade other people to read them. We are better known to the public for our bad manners than for graciousness.

While the bad image writers give us is appalling, even more distressing is the fact that the public in general never feels the authors have misrepresented us. The librarian in Brooklyn who never cared enough about Betty Smith to even look at her; the pinch-nosed librarian who kept the good books from the young people and reveled in gossip in *The Sound and the Fury;* Saroyan's librarian who bawled out Ulysses and his little friend for handling books they could not read; and the unspeakable librarian in Memphis who browbeat and degraded young Richard Wright, forcing him to lie and cheat in order to borrow a book from her white library.[1] And recently in poking fun at a California town where amazing things happened, a television talk-show host brought a laugh when he said the town idiot was the librarian. The new president of Johns Hopkins University said a college president has to generate an image that can engender confidence in the institution, be the kind of personality that makes people feel good about the university.

This is the kind of image we librarians, from directors to assistants, need to generate.

We have been true to you, Melvil Dewey, right down the line from ALA to our library schools, our administrators, and our individual staff members. Let's take them in order.

Like Gulliver, ALA is so tied down by its thousands of Lilliputian details of organization and so geared to the informational approach to librarianship that it has little time or interest in setting the pace or assuming the leadership that would influence the people of America to read and think and understand in these perilous times. Long ago ALA should have established a program on TV where books would be dramatized by highly qualified professionals as the BBC is doing currently. And now that the BBC is sending people flocking into libraries for the *Forsyte Saga* and books about Elizabeth I, Henry VIII, and Cousin Bette, why are these shows sponsored only by the Ford Foundation, Mobil Oil, and Xerox? Could not the nation's libraries have been mentioned as cosponsors? Did anyone at ALA care enough about the promotion of reading to investigate the matter? And if the BBC discontinues its dramatizations in the future, is it likely that ALA will some day institute such programs with the help of foundations and commercial sponsors? Not unless the promotion of reading attains a higher priority than ever before.

When the younger librarians set up the Social Responsibilities Round Table, it sounded hopeful but it never seemed to connect with books and reading. As I understand it, these librarians wanted libraries to take stands on social issues. As an individual, I belong to the League of Women Voters, Nader's organization, Common Cause, and the American Civil Liberties Union because I wish to stand with these people on social issues. As a librarian, I have fought the same battle with books. There are on our shelves thousands of books that fight against prejudice, overpopulation, inhuman prisons, injustice, mistreatment of children, and all the other evils of our society. If we librarians feel social responsibility, books are our weapons. Our social obligation is to read these books and see that society reads them. This is far more difficult than carrying banners and taking institutional stands on such causes as Gay Liberation.

Probably ALA is not entirely responsible, but it is interesting to note that workshops listed periodically in *American Libraries* are largely centered on technical processes and bibliographical matters. It seems fair to say that ALA in spirit and practice perpetuates Dewey's old idea of libraries with the addition of new gadgets.

Dewey's idea of the library is also perpetuated by library schools where the students are trained in the Dewey tradition rather than being prepared to meet this new day with its needs and challenges. Look at the curriculum of the modern library school: Descriptive Cataloging, Subject Cataloging and Classification, Advanced Classification, Indexing and Abstracting, Automation of Library Services, Reference and Bibliography, Advanced Reference and Bibliography, Government Documents, Research, Administration, Principles of Book Selection, one or two electives on materials for children, and, rarely, a course called "Materials for Adolescents." Not one course on how to work on the floor of the library with people, no attempt to encourage individual growth and self-development and certainly no wide reading of books. Should not every library school offer courses on making use of radio and TV? Should there not be a course in public speaking that would train the student to speak effectively of books in public? Where are the courses in public relations and methods of penetrating the community and selling the idea of reading? Why not a course in the teaching of remedial reading so disadvantaged adults might one day become our readers? Should not every library school in a city have a project operating on the streets, experimenting with ways of reaching the disadvantaged, with library students on its staff under the supervision of a creative expert? Some of the teachers in library schools who have not worked in a public library in twenty-five years have no conception of today's library patrons, of the difficulties to be met, and the needs to be filled. Kenneth Harrison, a British librarian who visited some thirteen American library schools, writes, "Is it really all that unreasonable that we practicing librarians should ask the deans and faculties to produce people well equipped to deal with readers on the library floor and not just Johnny-heads-in-the-air? Of course we want vision and thoughtfulness, but we want these qualities combined with know-how and practical approach. But on the subject of vision . . . it certainly is a commodity in short supply at the moment. But I am hopeful that the output of the library schools will provide us with more librarians of vision, for 'where there is no vision,' the people will perish."

In the six or so library schools where I have taught, many of the students who were attracted to librarianship because they loved books and people are appalled at the aridity of the courses. Recently the head of a library school and I were discussing the recent project where library school students were sent to ALA at the expense of a firm interested in libraries. The head of the school remarked, "When the students came back, they all reported the same old thing—how dissatisfied students from all the schools were with their courses." A few months back, I had a friendly but vociferous argument with the head of another library school. I pointed out to him with my usual tact that his curriculum was lopsided with not enough recognition for the promotion of reading. He came at me full force, and in about the tenth round, when we were both hanging on the ropes, he said he had two questions to ask me: 1) If he agreed to include courses on the promotion of reading, where did I think he would find teachers? 2) He had been visiting public libraries and had found them by and large pretty dismal and administered by librarians with squinted vision. If he trained assistants to be dynamic readers' advisors, what did I think would happen to them under these administrators? He won the match by a K.O. for I could answer neither question. I could not think of a public library in the entire United States that had sold books and reading to an entire community and endeared itself to its people as Joe Wheeler sold the Enoch Pratt Free Library to Baltimore. How few public libraries are administered by men or women with vision who develop and inspire their staffs to serve people as he did. Often in my classes I have had students with charm, dedication, a love of books and people, and high intelligence. I write of such a student, "This girl should go far if she comes under inspired supervision." I despair when I think how slim the chances are that such will be the case.

And this brings us to administrators. While there are some excellent administrators who are widely read, creative, and determined to make books meaningful to their communities, too many public librarians define their jobs as making Dewey's system work. The emphasis is on the system rather than the people of the community. As long as the staff is on duty in the building, the books in order on the shelves, questions are being answered, and no one is complaining to the mayor, the administrator often feels his job is being done. He feels he has provided a well-rounded book collection and if people want to read the books, they can come and get them. Besides, the staff is too busy with housekeeping matters and the daily routines to be out of the building talking to people about books, appearing on TV, or distributing book-lists and paperback books. Though service clubs or individuals might subsidize billboards or newspaper ads, he thinks it might be difficult to undertake. It may be as easy for the administrator to think up reasons for not rendering service beyond the call of duty to the public as it will be for the taxpayer to think up reasons for not straining himself to meet the librarian's budget requests.

But the most serious criticism of the administration and the public library is that, like Rip Van Winkle, they are stuck fast in yesterday. By and large, we have always laid out our buildings, selected our books, and allocated out staff for the middle-aged, middle class as we do today. Statistics tell us that by the end of the 1970s, over 50 per cent of the people in the United States will be under twenty-five. Yet most administrators either ignore work with young adults or, if they find it has been set up, boot it out, complimenting themselves all the while that the library "treats young people just like they do adults." This means ignoring them completely unless they ask for information. If YA work has not been abandoned and the administrator is a flaming liberal, one staff member is entitled the young adult librarian while all the rest of the staff are designated adult librarians. Go in any library and four out of five of the patrons will probably be teenagers; but four out of five of the staff will be adult librarians who are made to feel there is more status in serving adults even if they are not alive to be served. Should the administrator be realistic enough to establish YA work and provide young adult librarians who distinguish themselves as readers' advisors, these YA librarians will be promoted to be branch librarians, for if an assistant distinguishes himself as a readers' advisor, he reaches a dead end in his specialty. The only way up is in administering the system. Influencing young people to read and think has a limited future in the public library.

As for changing library schools and administrators, it is like an irresistible force meeting an immovable object. The administrator says he could never promote reading with the technically trained graduates of library schools and the library schools say if they produced readers' advisors, administrators would not employ them for they are looking for people with technical training. So library schools will continue to produce technicians—just what administrators want.

In the past the librarian was considered one of the community's important citizens. By and large, he was permitted to run the public library about as he saw fit, but not anymore. In these times of crises, where money is in very short supply, the librarian seated in his office administering a genteel staff of mechanics may become as extinct as the great auk. The public library of the future could be one large computer with answers to questions—presided over by a few computer stuffers.

If the public library is to survive, it will have to demonstrate that it makes a difference in the quality of life in the community. People must regard their libraries as oases in these critical times where an inspired, widely read staff permeates the community to introduce people— through books—to ideas, concern for society, inspiration, and delight. It is not enough that Melvil Dewey put the books in order on the shelves. We must take them down, read them, and give them to the people.

# APPENDIX A

# *The Tool Shed*

While chapters in the body of this book deal with the aims and goals of work with young adults, this appendix contains tools, i.e., instructions, lists, and suggestions designed to give public and school librarians new to YA work, and possibly future library-school teachers, practical pointers for promoting reading among adolescents.

## BOOK SELECTION

The best books for young adults are the books that most truly interpret to them the process of living.* Since the adolescent clientele of the school and public libraries ranges from the most deprived and apathetic to the most fortunate and accelerated, it is necessary to use a sliding scale in selecting the best books for the various readers to be served. However, there are yardsticks for measuring creative writing that are as applicable to book selection for young adults as for adults.

Fiction should conform to the following principles:

*1. It should interpret life truly.*

The story should not be sensational, exaggerated, prettied up, or distorted. A realistic picture of the adult world, even if frankly written, may not be as harmful as books that make life seem too easy and too

---

*Appendix B reflects the selection policies of the Enoch Pratt Library when Edwards was the Coordinator of Work with Young Adults. *Ed.*

happy, and so do not prepare young people to understand the problems of maturity. The best books do not end like fairy tales, where after all dragons are slain the handsome hero and beautiful heroine marry and live happily ever after. People are neither all good nor all bad. Most problems are not easy to solve. In well-written books people may suffer intensely at times and sorrow and despair are mingled with triumph and joy. If one looks about him at the people he knows, he will see few perfectly happy, healthy, well-adjusted individuals. He will see injustice prevail on occasion and the innocent suffering for the guilty. He may see fairly ordinary people rise to great heights of nobility and the superintendent of the Sunday school embezzling the bank's funds. In other words, life is complex and the writer who makes it appear too pat or too ugly or too beautiful—the writer who oversimplifies—is probably not painting a true picture.

*Caution:* Librarians who select books for young adults must guard with equal care against mistaking realistic writing for cheapness and cheap writing for realism.

*2. The characters should be real and vital.*

They should react to situations in the story as they would in real life. In many of the best novels the events related work a change in a character over a long period of time and after much soul-searching. Willie Keith in *The Caine Mutiny* [Wouk, 1954] changed from a mama's boy to a man after months aboard an old minesweeper in the Pacific during World War II. It took considerable time for Anna Karenina to change from a brilliant figure in Russian society to a despairing suicide. Willa Cather's Antonia became a fulfilled woman after a long, lonely childhood and youth. All these transformations are credible. Too sudden a change is no more convincing in a novel than it is in real life. Characters in books should react very much like their counterparts in real life who share a similar heredity and environment. In this connection it might be said that novels of plot written with the idea of spinning a good yarn are welcome entertainment and diversion as long as their characters react as normal human beings. But the best novels do more than recount events; they show how these events change the characters. Young people prefer novels with sound characters developed from action and dialogue rather than from long explanatory passages.

*3. Selection should be based on awareness of the world today, an understanding of modern youth, and common sense.*

Books containing realistic passages, whether they be creative works of fiction or factual nonfiction should be included in young-adult collections if the dominant theme of the book contributes to an understanding of life and if the questionable passages contribute to the development of the theme or the portrayal of character. When A. B. Guthrie wrote his magnificent *The Big Sky*, which had been researched carefully and was wonderfully true to life, there was fear that innocent teenagers might realize that this untamed mountain man shacked up with his beloved Teale Eye without hunting up a minister on the vast empty plains; that the baby was blind because of his past indiscretions; that he killed his best friend in a jealous rage. So the publishers brought out a cleaned-up edition for young people. *The Cruel Sea* suffered the same fate and was redone without the women and sex, carrying on its jacket the blessing of a highly placed English divine. If these two fine books in their original form are too hot for the timid librarian to handle, he does not have to purchase them. But it is not fair to the youngsters to make these virile books neuter. Let's not drape the nude Greek statues in the park. I am amazed that many school libraries in Guthrie's native state do not stock his distinguished novels.

Young people today, exposed as they are to the mass media and sophisticated as they are in their personal associations, are not likely to be upset by frank writing. When a character in a book uses "objectionable" language, the reader or reviewer should ask himself, "Is this what that character would say under the circumstances? Do I understand the character and the story better for the language used and the situations depicted? Does the book ring true?" If the answer to these questions is "Yes," there is no reason to condemn the book. It is the responsibility of librarians to show young people how to read such books with understanding rather than to deprive adolescents of them. It is easier to underestimate than to overestimate the ability of teenagers to understand books written for adults. Time spent hunting objectionable words and making lists of books to ban might be employed to better advantage in searching for books to enrich and delight young readers. And let us bear in mind Mayor Jimmy Walker's observation that "no girl was ever ruined by a book."

*4. Dull, didactic books, no matter how informative or how lofty the author's intentions, should be excluded from recreational collections for young adults.*

*5. Books written with a bias intended to persuade the reader of a religious or political point of view are out of place in recreational collections in public and school libraries.*

*6. Moralistic writing that seeks to drive home a lesson should be passed over in favor of more subtle stories.*

Some teenage novels do give youngsters sound advice but in an entertaining way. What is referred to here is the dull book concerned more with sin than good sense.

*7. Interpretive writing that depicts the human heart is more useful in stimulating thinking and developing understanding than is factual information on the same subject, though both types of writing may be useful.*

As has been said, pamphlets and books proving scientifically that all races are fundamentally the same are not as effective as novels and biographies that cause the reader to identify with the people of other races. Of course, young people with a scientific bent may prefer to read pure science and they should be encouraged to seek out bibliographies and refer to the catalog.

*8. Titles that seem adequate but are no better than books on the same subject already in stock should be rejected unless the demand for that type of book exceeds the supply.*

*9. Books that present any racial or national group in a derogatory manner, that consistently use objectionable nicknames for ethnic groups or races, that perpetuate stereotyped racial characteristics and ideas, are not acceptable.*

*10. Fiction written especially for the teenager does not need to be judged by the standards set up for adult novels.*

As I have said, teenage books that teach the apathetic the love of reading, that satisfy the younger adolescent's emotional and psychological needs and throw light on his problems, are tools that the skillful librarian uses to develop readers. They are acceptable if the characters, dialogue, problems, and situations are credible, if there is a sound code of behavior and morals, if they are in good taste and reasonably well written.

In a sports story, for instance, the reader usually wants an accurate play-by-play account of the crucial part of the game plus the reasoning that leads the hero to make the plays he does. In addition to action there must be suspense, drive, and purpose—the outcome must matter a great deal to the reader as well as the players.

*11. Style that distinguishes a book as literature is very rare. Though it is to be cherished when found, it is not essential.*

It is difficult to transmit to young people an appreciation of style for it is an elusive concept to grasp. Few adults appreciate style in many fields of art; many people have no comprehension of it at all. In many American homes the pictures on the walls portray a little golden-haired girl and her Collie dog or the old mill wheel. The most raucous music depicting the self unbuttoned appeals to more people than Beethoven's symphonies. Many of us with two college degrees cannot detect style in modern art or poetry. If we belabor the point of appreciating literary style, we may confuse young people unnecessarily. If we recommend only the best-written books and look down on those they can enjoy, we may undermine their pleasure in reading. Besides, it is far more important to awaken in young people a social consciousness than to insist that they appreciate style. *Black Like Me* is more meaningful for most of them than a novel by Thackeray.

The experienced reviewer has a kind of built-in Geiger counter that ticks loudly when his eye passes over writing of exceptional quality. The story may be as tough as Hemingway's *The Killers,* as polished as Cather's *Death Comes for the Archbishop,* or as gay [carefree] as Marquis' *Archy and Mehitabel* [1950]—but the originality, truth, and grace of the writing will, as Clifton Fadiman put it, set bells ringing inside the sensitive reader.

*12. The principles and standards of book selection should determine the books to be included in the collection rather than one's individual taste or pressure from citizens, however well meaning.*

In any given year one may not find five novels that pass all the tests cited above. One judges books as he does people by weighing faults against virtues. He decides in the end whether a book is worth buying despite its faults or is unacceptable despite its virtues—after reading the entire book, not after passing judgment on a few passages read out of context. One must be sure his conclusions are based on sound reasoning uninfluenced by personal feelings. Even so, no one's judgment is infallible.

### *Points to Be Considered in Judging Nonfiction*

*1. The date of publication is especially important for history, travel, vocational, and similar books.*

Even in sports the rules change and once-famous players are forgotten. In certain fields of science a book three years old may contain unreliable statements and should be discarded.

*2. How much of an authority is the author?*

Diet and psychiatry are but two fields about which misleading information is published.

*3. What is the author's point of view?*

Race relations, civil rights, juvenile delinquency, and the draft can be approached from various angles.

*4. Has the book vitality?*

Many books pass all the other tests but become a drug on the market because they fail to interest the reader.

*5. As was said of fiction, titles that seem adequate but are no better than those already in stock should be rejected unless there is a need for more books on the subject.*

Various authors may write a biography of the same person, but two biographies of any individual are usually quite enough. It is easy to overstock on such subjects as ballet, insects, the North Pole, or other subjects that are of interest to only a very few readers. On the other hand, we should watch for books on subjects that might give our readers a new interest.

*6. A quick evaluation:*

In *Living with Books* [1935], from which many of these principles were borrowed, Helen Haines says that one can evaluate nonfiction quickly by noting the following: publisher, title page, introduction, chapter headings, readability. The first and last chapters often epitomize the purpose of the book. Read a controversial chapter. Note the style and references to sources of information. Test the index. The usefulness of a nonfiction title decreases if there is no index.

Some school library supervisors have set up ten tests of sound book-selection practice. Some of these were covered above, but they are listed here again:

1. Do you *read*—widely, regularly, critically?

2. Do you keep a running file of order cards based on your own reading, suggestions from teachers and students, and needs uncovered by use of the library?

3. Do you check books by reading reviews in accepted sources?

4. Is there a written statement of book-selection policy for your school?

5. Do you apply well-defined criteria for the book that you choose?

6. Do you select books in relation to a well-thought-out plan for the development of the total collection?

7. Do you consider school needs and pupil interests and abilities when choosing books?

8. Do you encourage wide participation in book selection?

9. Do you examine books before buying them whenever possible?

10. Do you compare related books to see which is preferable?

In *Books, Young People and Reading Guidance* [G. R. Hanna and M. K. McAllister, 1960], Hanna discusses book selection and sums up the matter by saying, "The librarian seeks to provide the most useful and at the same time, the most satisfying books at the highest literary level compatible with usefulness."

Book selection should be position rather than negative. The librarian who works with teenagers is more obligated to stimulate thinking and hand on our cultural heritage than to protect young people from life's realities. The book that leads a teenager from consideration of himself to concern for all men should be made not only available, but interesting to adolescents by being shelved in inviting collections and vitalized by outgoing librarians.

## BOOK LISTS

A book list should be so designed that anyone who picks it up will be impelled to open it and see what is inside. Some librarians today are designing stunning lists for young adults, but not all. The best ones have such illustrations as a long, wicked-looking red car, a trumpet player, a reproduction of a clever drawing by a professional artist—whatever fits a vital subject and appeals to today's teenagers. The worst ones feature a teenage boy and girl looking as if they had just come from a meeting of the Youth for Clean Living Club. They are often seated, reading a book together, though the more daring depict the couple seated, leaning back to back and reading their separate books. A variation on this is the "upward and onward" theme—the climb up the mountain, the boy reaching down to give the girl a hand while clutching his book.

The same principles for illustrations and captions given in the section on displays hold good here. However, if the cut used on the cover is self-explanatory, a caption is not needed. For instance, a book list on the brotherhood of man has been put out with nothing on the cover but the reproduction of a *New Yorker* cartoon showing a hippie carrying a sign with the inscription "Dig Thy Neighbor." It is necessary to get permission from the publisher to use a cut from copyrighted material. This is, as a rule, not difficult to obtain. Since posters are not published, permission to enlarge a cut from published material and use it on a poster is not necessary.*

Most effective lists feature one subject, but there is more need for general lists than for general displays. Vacation reading lists distributed through the schools at the end of the school year are an excellent way of contacting the teenagers of a community. For either the public or school library, attractive lists will help establish good public relations and advertise the library as well as promote reading.

A school library might put out numerous bookmarks throughout the school year, tying the book to the school's activities. When the school play is given, bookmarks could be distributed featuring the cast of characters on one side and plays, biographies, and stagecraft on the other. For each of the school sports the bookmark might feature the season's schedule on one side and sports books on the other. Dances, a special speaker, assembly programs, and other activities could be tied to books in the library in this way. A library club could be responsible for this activity.

Unless lists are published in quantities over ten thousand, they can be produced very attractively and fairly inexpensively on a multilith machine. Either colored or white paper can be used; the color of the paper, the color of the ink, the format of the lists, the illustration on the cover, and the caption should all be in harmony.

Once the list has been printed, one should make it available in quantity and create a demand for it instead of storing the supply in a cupboard and handing the lists out gingerly. Lists should be put out where people can pick them up in the branches of a city system. They should be handed out on classroom visits, at book fairs, at teenage club meetings—wherever they would be welcomed. Then if requests for books on the list pour in, extra copies of the titles in demand can be ordered.

---

*The author is interpreting the fair use principle that guides the use of published materials broadly. These views are not supported wholly by the publisher. While the intent in this example is not commercial, each case must be weighed individually and against all aspects of the fair use principle. *Ed.*

## ANNOTATION WRITING

If we design a list so attractive that anyone who sees it will pick it up, it is important that he not put it down when he reads the annotations or because there are no annotations. Simply listing authors and titles under various headings is better than nothing but it does not give the reader any indication of which titles would appeal to him and which would bore or baffle him. Below are sample annotations taken from published lists for young adults that illustrate the difference between a merely adequate annotation (a) and one written with art (b).

*The King Must Die*    Mary Renault

(a) The Theseus legend is vividly and dramatically retold in this story.

(b) Theseus steps from the realm of legend to enter the bull ring, thread the labyrinth with its minotaur, win Ariadne, and challenge the matriarchy of his day.

*Johnny Tremain*    Esther Forbes

(a) When an injury to his hand changed the life of a silversmith's apprentice, he found his own role to play in the beginnings of the American Revolution.

(b) Struggling Johnny Tremain, having lost his trade and birthright, finds himself involved in mysterious tea parties, firebrand politics, and secret meetings with Paul Revere, Sam Adams, and John Hancock.

*Brave New World*    Aldous Huxley

(a) In a highly satirical vein, Huxley pictures Utopia, scientific and industrialized. His predictions are bitter and forceful.

(b) In a world where science has solved all mankind's problems— where there is no pain, hunger, suffering, or freedom (none is needed)—one test-tube baby has dangerous thoughts about freedom and individuality.

Annotation writing is an art. Here are a few pointers, some of which were originally stated by Helen Haines in *Living with Books* and still hold true:

1. In most lists for young adults, an annotation should not run over about thirty-five words.

2. Try to write the annotation in one sentence, as two or more tend to give a jerky rather than a flowing rhythm.

3. Avoid too many adjectives. Instead of saying the story is interesting or delightful or exciting, use nouns and verbs to tell what was interesting or delightful or exciting.

4. The active voice is better than the passive.

5. The best annotations for young adults get moving with the first words. Somebody should be doing something, if possible.

6. Direct action can be varied with a statement that catches the attention. (See annotation (b) for *Brave New World*.)

7. Do not give the story away.

8. Do not overrecommend the book.

9. Include statements that place the book in its proper time and place.

10. After copy for a list is completed, read the annotations aloud. Awkward expressions, too frequent use of the same word, and other inelegancies can be avoided this way.

11. Only occasionally begin annotations with *A* and *The*.

12. Never use the word *you*. This word is overly familiar and gives an annotation a hortatory, saving-the-reader-for-democracy tone that is highly objectionable. All annotations should be written as if for adults, without condescension or a patronizing tone.

13. Do not repeat the title or any information it gives.

*The librarian's annotation tells:*

1. What the book is about and how it ends
2. The setting and period covered
3. Literary qualities
4. Usefulness
5. Limitations
6. To whom it will appeal
7. How it compares with other books in the field

The necessary bibliographic information should appear under the author and title at the head of the card. The annotation need not be confined to one sentence but should be written in a flowing style and should not exceed about fifty words, as longer annotations necessitate two review cards and crowd library files. One should keep in mind that this is not so much a literary exercise as a buying guide to tell a librarian whose funds are probably low whether or not the book reviewed will be a good investment.

## BOOK TALKS

*The objectives of giving book talks to teenagers are:*

1. To sell the idea of reading for pleasure
2. To introduce new ideas and new fields of reading
3. To develop appreciation of style and character portrayal
4. To lift the level of reading by introducing the best books the audience can read with pleasure
5. To humanize books, the library, and the librarian

Anyone without an emotional problem or a speech difficulty can talk about books effectively if he wants to badly enough, if he is enthusiastic about books and wishes to share his pleasure in them, and if he is well prepared.

There are various ways of giving book talks and any speaker can measure the effectiveness of his method by the number of young people who come to the library to borrow the books spoken about.

One method of preparing a talk is to select a dramatic incident from a book about which one is enthusiastic. The incident should have plot and continuity enough to hold an audience, and preferably, should not occur at the end of the book. Introduce the characters and tell only enough of the story leading up to the incident selected to make the talk intelligible. If the incident to be related is in the first person, it can be changed to the third or left as it is written and introduced by some such remark as, "This is the way Jane Eyre tells what happened." The typed copy of the talk should run approximately four and a half pages, double-spaced, as a general rule. Read the prepared talk aloud for its sound and style. Do not point out lessons or use a hortatory tone. Do not end with "If you want to know what happened, read the book" or leave the audience dangling. Challenge an accelerated class at times by telling them the book to be presented demands thought and concentration.

Whether one memorizes a talk or not, he should type it as it is intended to be given. There are two reasons for this: (1) If the talk is given some months later, one will not have to reread the book but merely the typed talk. (2) Over the years one can build up an extensive repertoire of successful talks to be given to new classes. As books go out of print or lose their appeal, book talks based on them should be discarded for it is important that the books talked about be available and have strong appeal to the current generation.

Few people speak well extemporaneously. Words do not come to them quickly enough and they seem disorganized, halting, and self-conscious. By reading over a typed talk many times, a speaker can be sure of the order of events to be related and appropriate words will come to him easily. Since the author's language usually has a fluidity few amateurs can attain, it is well to use his words as much as possible, supplying needed interpolation and cutting as necessary. After many presentations of the talk the speaker will unconsciously have memorized it just as he did "America" by singing it over several times. The sooner he memorizes the talk, the smoother his presentation will be.

### The Technique of Delivery

1. Do not begin to speak until the audience is ready to listen. Wait for attention with good humor. Create a favorable impression of yourself quickly and unobtrusively without a hostile stare or a rap for order.

2. State clearly the author and title of the book. In addition, if possible, distribute a list of titles to be presented in either thumbnail sketches or book talks. The list might be captioned "Speaking of Books," and if long, broken up into interest sections such as: "To Keep You Up at Night," "For the Nonconformist," "Geared to a Man's Taste," "For the Female of the Species," "Current Happenings."

3. Be sure everyone in the room can hear all that is said.

4. Bring the story to life so vividly that the speaker disappears and only the story lives. Any gesture or tone that enhances the story is right; anything that calls attention to the speaker is wrong. Almost any planned gesture is a mistake.

5. Change the pace of speaking to suit the tempo of the story.

6. Vary the tone. For excitement a low tone is best—a tense whisper is more effective than a yell.

7. For emphasis the pause is essential. For example, "He looked down the well and saw [pause, take a breath through the mouth, expanding the diaphragm] a *hand* sticking out of the water."

8. When two characters are conversing look to the right for one, to the left for the other, and throughout the talk keep them in the same relative positions. When Jane Eyre speaks to Mr. Rochester

she should look directly into his eyes, not out the window. Since he is taller than she, she will look up a bit. Mr. Rochester, who is standing opposite her, will look to the left if she looked to the right and will look down a bit, directly into her eyes but not at the floor, when he is talking to her. Between their remarks the speaker looks at the audience for "he said" or "she replied," as these words are not part of the conversation between the two main characters.

9. Stand firmly without rocking. Never back off from an audience unless you wish to indicate fear or hesitancy.

10. *Never* apologize to the audience for yourself. If you were able to drag yourself to the platform or into the classroom, make a final effort and look glad to be there.

11. Do not read to an audience if it can be avoided. The minute you take your eyes from them you decrease the intensity of their attention. Even a talk on poetry is a hundred times more effective if memorized and recited with one's eyes on the audience. Always look at the audience.

12. Do not indulge in nervous gestures. How many librarians have straightened out paper clips as they spoke! Keep your hands out of the picture unless they are helping to tell the story.

13. Do not pretend to have read books you have not read.

14. The face should reflect the feelings of the speaker. An expressionless face cuts the audience off from sharing with the speaker the emotions generated by the book. The eyes, face, and hands make the difference between a tape recording and a book talk.

15. Undue emphasis on *a* and *the* make a talk sound memorized. These articles are pronounced with the sound of the short *u* and elided into the next word, i.e., "uboy," "thusong."

16. The feet can indicate a change of scene or the passing of time. As one recounts the events of an exciting battle at night, he stands with feet normally close together with his weight on the ball of one foot. As the last bomb drops and the battle ends, the speaker stops speaking, relaxes, moves his free foot to the side, and shifts his weight to it. Not until the other foot comes to rest in its normal new position does the speaker begin to tell what happened the next morning. Thus the audience has a chance to shift to a new place and time.

17. Watch for boredom. If you selected a love story and chairs are beginning to squeak and there is some coughing, make a quick

change. Do not scold the audience or let them know you realize all is not going well. Say something like "Well, to make a long story short, she broke up with the city boy and married her cousin's friend. But let me tell you about Douglas Bader, the legless aviator in the R.A.F."

18. If it is possible to record a talk on a tape recorder and hear it played back, one can see where a change of tempo, a shorter or longer pause, or more variation in tone would improve delivery.

19. The public librarian visiting the school should speak in the library if possible and make the fullest use of the books in it, assembling the books to be talked about and allowing time for the students to check them out. Whether the talks are made by the school or the public librarian, it is often a good idea to stop talking ten minutes before the end of the period and encourage browsing.

20. A book talk is more effective when given to small rather than large groups. An audience of one class numbering around thirty is a group with which one can usually establish the good rapport more likely to lead to reading.

Remember, the librarian who gives books talks is not on trial as a performer but as a promotor of reading and his effectiveness should be judged by the amount of reading done as a result of his talks.

Book talks to classes or groups are effective in themselves but a class visit to the library can be something special if the librarian selects a subject or a theme and introduces it by making use of realia, music, posters, or films. From people living in the community, from travel agencies, consulates, teachers, and the teenagers themselves, one may borrow interesting collections, art objects, jewelry, costumes of other countries and other times. Artistic displays, a book talk, and a film in conjunction with the introduction of books on the subject can make a class visit to the library a memorable experience.

## BOOK DISCUSSIONS

Whoever undertakes to lead a book discussion has homework to do. He must read the book to be discussed carefully, noting passages that throw light on the author's purpose or show motivation of character or express a point of view that seems important. In his mind there should be a clear idea of the book's theme. What is the author saying about his main character or characters? How good is the writing? Is the book really true to life? What are its limitations? Professional reviewers often point out interesting matters for consideration that may not occur to the discussion leader. If the book is not new, outstanding critics may have written essays about it. After thorough preparation one should formulate three or four questions likely to provoke thought and bring out differences of opinion.

If one is leading a group discussion with teenagers, the ice can be broken by asking first, "If you had this book under your arm and a friend asked you what it was about, how would you tell him without being long-winded and tiresome and without giving away the ending?" Three or four might have a try at this. If the book under discussion were Maugham's *Of Human Bondage* and no really inspired answer were forthcoming, the leader might suggest that it is the story of a fellow with a clubfoot trying to find out what he wanted to be and do who got hung up with the wrong girl.

Some provocative questions likely to lead to a spirited discussion might be: "Why did Philip Carey stay with Mildred so long when he knew she was wicked and cruel?" "If you were a psychiatrist and had Philip on the couch, what would you say was bugging him?" "How would you predict his future? Will he be happy or not? Why?" "Was Philip in any way a typical young man?"

Often by playing devil's advocate the leader can so provoke people who had intended to sit and listen that they will plunge into the discussion. He should not overplay this role but should generate an air of excitement about the book and inject enough humor to amuse the audience when the argument becomes tense. In the end he should attempt to make a summary statement about the book on which all can agree, but if there is a sharp difference of opinion, he should sum up both sides, bringing in the opinion of professional critics as well as his own. He should, however, assure the audience that his opinion carries no more weight than anyone else's. The leader's role is to provoke thought and discussion and not to settle the matter once and for all.

The same technique can be used with a class of library-school students. This is also a good way to teach the application of the principles of book selection. If from one to three students report on a title read and discuss it in this way with the instructors and if the discussion is lively, many others will feel compelled to read the book and "get with it."

## DISPLAYS

Every year when autumn leaves fall, out come the posters featuring autumn leaves in school and public libraries over the country. The poster is usually entitled "Fall Reading." As cold weather sets in "Fall

Reading" is changed to "Winter Reading," illustrated with a picture of someone in an armchair in front of a fireplace reading while snow falls outside. "Spring Reading" usually features a row of paper jonquils, while "Keep Cool with a Book" shows a girl reading in a hammock with a cool drink within reach. These displays save a lot of shelving, as almost any book can be tossed in the collection beneath the poster, but they are corny and ineffective. They do no more than brighten up some corner a bit and call attention to reading. The young person who sees them in the library gets no message.

Displays are more effective if they feature a single concrete idea under such captions as "Damsels in Distress" (Gothic novels); "Music and All That Jazz"; "Growing Up Black"; "Laugh-In"; "Profiles in Courage"; "How Do I Love Thee." Whatever the subject for display, it is quite important that it be relevant to the teenager's world. Books on the subject should be directly under the poster, and if possible, lists related to the subject should accompany the display and be made available in quantity.

There should be an illustration that will catch attention and work with a striking caption to sell an idea. One strong illustration is better than two or three; don't gild the lily with a lot of little doodads that may be clever but clutter up the display and divert attention from the subject presented. Avoid the hortatory upward-and-onward tone in both caption and illustration as well as the use of the word *you*. A clever cartoon that elicits a laugh can drive home a point more effectively than a heavy-handed effort to be instructive. Two examples come to mind. A cartoon from the *Saturday Review* featured a kangaroo mother carrying quite a sizable offspring in her pouch and saying to him, "Don't you think it's about time you got yourself a job?" The Pratt Library used this on a list entitled "From High School to a Career." Another from the same magazine showed a caveman sitting, waiting his turn outside the Patent Office, clutching a wheel. This illustrated a list called "Science in Fact and Fiction." Cartoons in such magazines as the *Saturday Review of Literature* and *The New Yorker*, collections of commercial art, a book of designs, a clever ad, and various other sources can supply many ideas. When possible, cut out an illustration that looks promising and file it for future reference. Otherwise make a note describing the cut and indicating where it is located and include the note in the file of illustrations to be used for displays. This saves endless searching later and makes it possible to plan a plentiful supply of posters as they are needed. In selecting the cuts keep in mind that simple line drawings are easier to reproduce than complicated illustrations or halftones.

By removing one shelf from a section of shelves, a perfect location that has the effect of a stage can be provided for a display. If the poster to be used does not completely fill the rear space, cover the space with colorful pasteboard that complements the design of the poster and then attach the poster to this background. Amateurish lettering can spoil an otherwise artistic display—use the different types of ready-made letters that are available.

Displays should be changed often. If one plans six months ahead and prepares the posters likely to be useful, he will be able to introduce a variety of books to many readers. If only a very few books are borrowed a week after the display is put up, the librarian should be skeptical of its effectiveness. If the books are still there after two weeks, take the display down. For that matter, even a good display can be replaced in two or three weeks. There is no point in displaying books already in great demand, such as teenage romances, as the supply of titles will soon be exhausted and no one will have received a new idea for reading or stimulation to broaden his horizon.

If one is searching for inspiration for a new display, it is a good idea to find a telling illustration first, then plan a display around it. Otherwise one may select a subject, civil rights, for instance, and have to search for days before finding a cut that is not preachy or dull. It is better to keep ideas you wish to promote in the back of your head and collect appropriate cuts over a period of time, filing them to be used as needed.

Be sure there are readable books available in sufficient quantity on the topic to be featured if the promotion of recreational reading is the purpose of the display. There is not a large enough supply of books about Hawaii or the South Pole or motorcycles to justify a display of recreational reading on these subjects. Do not crowd such a display with books of information that the librarian himself would not care to read. Do not include classics just because they are classics. What high-school boy wants to read *Captains Courageous* [Kipling, 1897]? And many of them can get along without *Two Years Before the Mast* [Dana, 1840]. In this connection, do not use the displays to circulate books that just sit on the shelves. Young people must come to feel that if a book is on display, it must be good. Otherwise we will slow down the development of the reader by losing his confidence in our recommendations.

The school librarian would do well to ask his principal at the beginning of the school year to assign to the library a talented art student who will be given a school letter at the end of the year for service to the library. This student might be treated as a specialist and assigned only art work. The librarian should feel responsible for subjects for display, illustrations, and captions, while the student will do the actual preparation. Student suggestions should be welcome but the librarian must see that the posters have tone and quality, and if possible, a new twist rather than a cliché-ridden approach.

The display should amuse or pique the curiosity of the observer who, moving in for a closer look, will find his hand on a book ready to be borrowed.

## PAPERBACKS

When paperbacks first appeared they were, as a rule, pulps. The more innocuous were set in the Wild West and were trite and sensational. The cruder titles emphasized crime and sex, depicting on their covers women in some stage of undress or in intimate scenes with virile, handsome men—as someone has said, there was a pretty girl on the jacket and no jacket on the pretty girl. How publishers discovered there was more money to be made by turning to better literature jacketed with better taste is not known, but they did change. Could it be possible that publishers improved the tone of their covers because in those days, when a parent's disapproval carried some weight, they did not wish to stir up parental opposition to their youngsters purchasing these books? Some people are not fully aware of the change in both quality and appearance of paperbacks and still feel that readers of taste avoid these upstarts of the publishing world and read only hard-cover books. This point of view represents the horse-and-buggy stage of reading promotion and is a thoughtless refusal to use one of the librarian's most effective weapons against reluctance to read. If one looks through *Paperbacks in Print*, he will find an abundance of enriching reading, much of it to be had for less than one dollar per volume. Hundreds of the titles are on standard lists for young adults.

There are psychological reasons not clearly understood for the surprising appeal of paperbacks. It may be their size—they are so easy to carry about. People may think a book in paperback is an abridgement that will take less time to read than the hard-cover version. In a few cases this is true, but by and large the paperback publisher has bought the copyright from the original publisher and reprinted the book in toto without margins. Whatever the reasons, it is a known fact that people generally will read a book in paperback that they have passed over in hard cover. Such an excellent book as *Act One* may sit indefinitely on the shelves in hard cover to be snatched up and read as a paperback.

Teenagers are especially enthusiastic over paperback books. Macy's department store in New York City made the pockets of blue jeans

---

The section "Paperbacks" is more interesting for its view of the paperback novel in 1974 than for instructions on the use of paperbacks by librarians and teachers today. Nevertheless, for people generally interested in the evolution of books, these comments should prove enlightening. *Ed.*

larger to fit paperbacks, yet some librarians argue that they cannot fit paperbacks into their budget because they wear out so fast. A strong case can be made for the opposite point of view. Paperbacks are not expensive until they are cataloged and processed. Librarians have a consuming passion to do things to books. (It has been said that we do everything to a book but read it.) If they purchase a paperback, it seems to them unthinkable not to classify it, catalog it, provide it with a catalog card, make a shelf list card, file the cards, and stamp the secret code on a certain page. Then when the book is withdrawn they do it all over again, but backwards as in the TV ad where the tired woman's nerves unravel like a rope until she takes Anacin and the rope rewinds itself. Certainly this process is essential for books in hard cover and for the more expensive, original paperbacks but it does not pay off for a recreational collection. If there is already a card in the catalog for Smith's *A Tree Grows in Brooklyn* in hard cover, why not purchase additional copies in paperback, paste a book pocket with a book card in each, and call it square? At the Pratt Library the library stamp and the agency number are the only preparations applied. All paperbacks are checked on the electric charging machines with a dummy card marked *one miscellaneous charge,* and if the book is not returned, no messenger is sent. It has even been argued that it is cheaper for the library to give paperbacks away and let people return them if they wish rather than to circulate them in the regular way.

By the time we do all the things we can do to a paperback, we run the price up about $1.50 per copy, according to ALA figures. If we lose one of the books that was not cataloged, we will have lost about sixty cents. Had we cataloged the book, we would have lost $2.10. Of course, if the paperback is the only edition of a title, there is need for a card in the catalog to indicate the holding.

Let's look at it this way, *To Kill a Mockingbird* in hard cover originally cost $4.95. The paperback cost sixty cents. From its first publication this novel was in great demand. Everyone was talking about it, and then a forthcoming movie was announced. Not only was the book popular, but it was also just what we had been looking for to depict the needless cruelty of prejudice. Any library concerned for young people and the public weal would have bought one copy of the book for teenagers. This first copy would have been in hard cover. When it became evident that one copy would circulate to only about thirteen readers in a year (if the loan period were four weeks and each reader kept the book for the time allowed), some duplication should have seemed essential. Another copy in hard cover processed for $1.50 would have cost $6.45 and would have supplied thirteen more readers. The same investment would have bought ten paperbacks with enough left over for ten cards and pockets and would have given 130 more teenagers the opportunity to read a moving novel of social significance when they wanted to read it. A delay of a year diminishes the desire to read any book. If we believe reading is enriching, the number of people we can reach with a meaningful book is important. For most books in heavy demand it would seem a good idea to purchase one title in hard cover and as many paperback duplicates as funds will allow.

If fifty circulations is the life expectancy of a hard-cover title of *To Kill a Mockingbird* and we pay $6.45 to get the book on the shelves, the cost per circulation is thirteen cents. If we pay sixty cents for the paperback and get only five circulations from it, the cost is twelve cents per circulation—that is, if we can free ourselves from the compulsion to process the paperback. Of course, many paperbacks circulate more than five times. Some librarians are enthusiastic about special jackets and reinforced covers for paperbacks. If the cost of the materials and time spent do more for the cause of reading than would a duplicate copy, it would seem justifiable, but the librarian should be sure that more important projects are not sacrificed in this use of time.

When a paperback book falls apart, if we have done nothing more than stamp the library's name on it and put a card and pocket in the back, all we have to do is toss the book into the wastebasket—there is no catalog card to pull, no shelf list to change. If any records of holdings are necessary, they can be made on p-slips with tallies and kept in a desk drawer. We worry over theft and loss, but as was said above, a sixty-cent loss is not so painful as a $6.50 loss. Actually we lose far more hard-cover titles than any of us wish to admit.

Libraries should do more advertising. TV properly utilized on a professional level could send prospective readers rushing to libraries. Why do we never see ads about libraries and books in newspapers or billboards advertising the public library? The paperback book is a form of reading promotion and pays its way as such, in addition to supplying reading material. However, the effectiveness of paperbacks is lost without the proper means of calling them to the reader's attention. Packed in shelves with only their spines showing, they do not catch the eye of the prospective reader.

In a collection for young adults paperbacks are best displayed on a revolving rack. Airports, bus stations, and newsstands realize people have a psychological urge to keep turning a rack to see what is displayed in each section. It is essential that paperbacks be placed so their covers catch the eye. In most libraries space is at a premium and there is no room for elegant stationary racks to be placed against the wall. The revolving rack should contain titles of a recreational nature only. Paperbacks on serious scientific theories, the development of the drama, the history of civilization, and so forth, should be processed as much as necessary and shelved with hard-cover books on the same subject. In fields of science where expensive books become obsolete in three or so years, it would save money to buy the books in paperback and shelve them with books in the same field, that is, if the paperback comes on the market in time to be useful. It might also be a good idea to use paperbacks to feel out demand in fields where we hope the students may be interested but have reason to doubt they will be.

There are machines on the market that dispense paperbacks for sale, but some of the companies selling the machines control book selection, making the machines impractical for young-adult and school librarians. If a suitable machine is purchased, it should not take the place of the rack which offers books free to all readers. The machine is for the convenience of those who cannot get a book from the library in time for an assignment because undue pressure has been put on its stock, and for those who wish to build up their personal libraries.

Paperbacks are here to stay. They are the most effective method of reading promotion since Gutenberg, and any librarian working with teenagers is not doing his best for them if he does not make use of them.

## THOUGHTS BENEATH A BO TREE
### (*Especially for School Librarians*)

Encyclopedias say that when My Lord Buddha sought to gain insight into life's meanings, he meditated in solitude under a Bo tree and experienced a spiritual awakening known as "the enlightment." Anyone planning to be a school librarian might do well to find a Bo tree and sit in meditation under its branches until he experienced "the enlightenment" on his life's vocation. He might ask himself what he hoped to accomplish as a high-school librarian and how he would set about to attain his goals.

Under the Bo tree the future librarian would decide that in whatever position he found himself, he would make his library the "Big L" in the thoughts of the student body and faculty of his high school. He would resolve never to appear as a frustrated, defeated librarian, making do with leavings and eliciting pity or sinking into anonymity. Whatever was blocking him, he would eventually remove by one means or another to ensure that the school was served as it should be served. He would resolve never to lose his temper or raise his voice or be short with any student. Above all, he would plan to read and read and read. He would keep his sense of humor functioning and stand before students and faculty as their friendly, capable readers' advisor, as well as the information resource of the school. He would not seek popularity and love, but rather respect as a person and a librarian.

Early in his first year at the school he would ask for a conference with the principal to which he would go armed with a book-selection policy he had written out. This policy would state clearly what he hoped to do for the school, his standards for book selection, his procedure for handling complaints, and his general thoughts on the administration of the library. By asking the principal to read the policy carefully to see if they could agree on it, he might go a long way in educating an indifferent principal on the role of the library in the school. After the principal agreed to the policy, the librarian should ask if he might present it to the faculty.

At the faculty meeting the librarian should appear smartly dressed, rested, and full of vitality and should use the occasion to present the book-selection policy—this time by discussing it rather than reading it, explaining how he hoped to serve the school, paying special attention to book selection and the problem of censorship, demonstrating what could be accomplished by book talks to classes, visits of classes to the library for a period, and the atmosphere of warm cordiality he hoped to maintain in the library. This would also be the time to ask for continual suggestions and advice from the faculty.

Thereafter he would make it his business to convince each member of the faculty that it would be to his advantage to make constant use of the library for himself and his classes. How many high-school librarians bemoan the indifference of faculty members in general to the library while pointing with pride to the few teachers who come in every morning to read the daily paper or chat. A resourceful librarian can "sell" the idea of using the library. A faculty indifferent to the library often reflects an inadequate librarian. Too often a teacher has no reason to feel the librarian is interested in his field or can tell him anything about it he does not already know. He is honestly not convinced that consulting the librarian would be fruitful. It is up to the librarian to give such a teacher a different point of view.

A friendly little gesture sometimes wins over a faculty member—asking advice, or when an interesting new book comes in, sending it to the teacher to review or just to enjoy. But the most effective way of gaining respect and cooperation is a demonstration of knowledge and ability. In the field of reading promotion one way of doing this is to invite a class to visit the library during a period either for an introduction to collateral reading for a unit to be studied or for recreational reading. Using realia, music, book lists, a bang-up book talk, and a film, the librarian can bring books and the library alive for the students and convince the teacher that the librarian can enrich the teaching of his subject.

The librarian sitting under the Bo tree would resolve not to appear shy and self-conscious. If the P.T.A. asked him to address their organization, he would jump at the chance and give them a thundering good talk on what the library was doing to enrich their children, possibly ending with an introduction of the student aides and a demonstration of their performance in the service of the library. The aides might even hand out bookmarks they had helped prepare featuring books for parents to read or suggestions for Christmas or graduation gifts. If the P.T.A. does not ask the librarian to talk, the librarian should volunteer.

If the librarian is not included on committees to plan units of study or to revise the curriculum, the explanation could be poor public relations. Possibly he has not convinced department heads that with his knowledge of books and students, he is essential to such a committee. And speaking of public relations, why are so many groups of library aides made up of the school's "lost dogs"? Too often the desk is manned by overly effeminate boys, bossy little girls, and "eager beavers." It seem that those who can are members of other school activities; those who can't are library aides. This may be good therapy but it is poor public relations. Certainly the librarian should take his share of the unattractive youngsters but it would be well to give the impression that poised, popular, creative young people wish to be attached to the library.

The librarian should have a conference with the principal before the aides are appointed. He should lay before the principal a plan to make the library doubly effective that would require truly outstanding student aides. The plan might include:

1. A library club where books are discussed and aides are taught to give book talks. From this training, qualified student speakers could go through the school, visiting classes to introduce books and selling the idea of reading for pleasure.

2. A regular column in the school paper advertising new books in the library.

3. Designing, reproducing, and keeping on hand a supply of bookmarks that would advertise the library and correlate reading and the school's activities, as was discussed in the section "Book Lists" above.

4. Planning and putting on a school assembly.

5. A book-reviewing, mimeographed periodical by and for teenagers on the order of *You're the Critic* described in the body of the book.

6. A P.T.A. program.

7. Keeping a paperback book rack stocked with up-to-date titles approved for young adults, from which books will circulate to all.

8. Buying a machine to dispense paperback books and putting students in charge of its operation and the handling of monies involved. If the machine is out of the question, other arrangements could be made for the sale of books which could be handled by the student aides.

9. A poll of the student body to determine the ten most popular books.

10. A faculty meeting in the library early in the year where the aides and the librarian would "model" the new books by parading them down a runway and remarking on them in the manner of a Dior fashion show.

If such a program were presented to teenagers with personality and creativity, it is quite likely they would want to have a part in it. These young people could make the library the dynamo of the school, and think what it would do for the students themselves.

Under the Bo tree the librarian should attempt to work out some way of getting cards held for nonpayment of fines back into the hands of their owners, for the students most in need of books and reading are the very ones whose cards are usually in the drawer at the desk. A librarian in a Baltimore high school in a deprived community gave all the cards back, canceling the fines. Then he set a fruit jar on his desk labeled "Conscience Money," meaning "Pay what you feel you can." The students evidently interpreted this to mean "If you feel guilty about something, a contribution would help." Whatever the explanation, he collected more money by fruit jar than he had by fines and everyone kept his card. He even invited the boys and girls to meet each other in the library during their lunch hours, and in the process of hosting the social hour sent most of his guests out with books. The conventional librarian who followed him almost lost her mind. Eventually she had better order and fewer readers.

The librarian should resolve that lessons given in the use of the catalog should not be the heart and soul of the library program—the only contact some students have with the library. Instead the student should remember the library for the books and films presented with such enthusiasm that he had fallen under their spell.

The librarian should work out the best possible relationship with the principal of the school. In the matter of book selection it is to be hoped that the supervising librarian for a large system would be in charge, but if the principal has the authority to make final decisions on the purchase and circulation of books for the school, the librarian should pray that he will have a first-hand knowledge of books and modern standards of selection and the moral courage to stand firm in a crisis. A prayer for a faculty with the same point of view might be in order.

If the faculty and principal should be overly conservative and unaware of standard practices, the librarian should work tactfully to bring them to a more liberal point of view. If the librarian were considering a frank, realistic new book for purchase, was convinced it belonged in the library, and has found support for it in standard tools, he should ask the principal to read it before he adds it to the collection. If he agrees the librarian might add the book, the librarian would look to him for support if complaints were made. But if the principal failed to stand firm and yielding to pressure, demanded that the librarian remove criticized books, the librarian should resign for every book the librarian removes proves him either incompetent for having added the book or a coward for removing it. Self-respect is in the balance. It is a good idea to nail down the new job before resigning, nor should one leave without quietly explaining to the principal why it was impossible to work under him any longer.

Another thought resulting from meditation under the Bo tree would be the importance of cooperating with the public library. All too often both public and school librarians have allowed petty jealousy of their individual territories to take precedence over the enrichment of the students. If public and school librarians joined forces and worked effectively together, they could triple or quadruple the results they accomplish working separately. Public librarians are sometimes indifferent and when they approach the schools are not well enough prepared. School librarians are inclined to consider the public librarian's visits an invasion of their territory. The public librarian who gives book talks in the schools should encourage the use of the school library and the circulation of its books, mentioning the public library as a second source. The school librarian should encourage the students to join the public library and to make use of its facilities. The two institutions should work hand in glove to develop each student to his full potential as a reader.

Finally, on graduation night, as each student walks across the stage the librarian should ask himself, "What contribution did I make to this student? Have I enlarged his vision and taught him the joy of reading? Have I made books so meaningful to him that he will read all his life, or have I just furnished him with information for assignments?"

## FILMS AND OTHER MEDIA

Anyone who has seen such films as *Two Men and a Wardrobe, The Occurrence at Owl Creek Bridge, Phoebe,* and *The Hand* knows that films have a great contribution to make to the enrichment, understanding, and delight of young adults.

In any book on library work with young adults there should be a discussion of films, records, and other media for they have become an important and meaningful part of the modern library's plans for the teenager. However, someone else will have to write of these wonderful new media since they reached their present high level of development after my retirement from the Pratt Library. Furthermore, I wish to stand primarily on my advocacy of the book.

## READING LIST

This list of books for young adults is really a suggested list for the beginning librarian to read in order that he may feel some assurance as he works with readers of varying age and ability. It is not inclusive, nor is it a list for all time, since many of the books will suffer the fate of Ozymandias. No two librarians would make identical lists, but each of these books has something to say to teenagers, and if given the right reader, will enrich and delight him.

A. For Younger Readers

| | |
|---|---|
| Anonymous | *Go Ask Alice* |
| Arundel | *The Longest Weekend* |
| Bonham | *Durango Street* |
| Cavanna | *Almost Like Sisters* |
| Colman | *Bride at Eighteen* |
| Craig | *It Could Happen to Anyone* |
| Decker | *Switch Hitter* |
| Felsen | *Crash Club* |
| Gilbreth | *Cheaper by the Dozen* |
| Hinton | *The Outsiders* |

| Hunt | *Up a Road Slowly* |
|------|--------------------|
| Hunter | *Soul Brothers and Sister Lou* |
| Mathis | *Teacup Full of Roses* |
| Norton (Andre) | Any title |
| Petry | *Tituba of Salem Village* |
| Stolz | *Pray Love, Remember* |
| Werbsa | *The Dream Watcher* |
| Wolff | *A Crack in the Sidewalk* |
| Zindel | *My Darling, My Hamburger* |
| Zindel | *The Pigman* |

## B. Useful Titles for Transferring the Reader to Adult Books

| Asimov | *Fantastic Voyage* |
|--------|--------------------|
| Brontë | *Jane Eyre* |
| Clarke | *2001: A Space Odyssey* |
| Du Maurier | *Rebecca* |
| Frank | *Diary of a Young Girl* |
| Freedman | *Mrs. Mike* |
| Graham | *Dove* |
| Green | *I Never Promised You a Rose Garden* |
| Griffin | *Black Like Me* |
| Gunther | *Death Be Not Proud* |
| Head | *Mr. & Mrs. Bo Jo Jones* |
| Heyerdahl | *Kon-Tiki* |
| Hilton | *Lost Horizon* |
| Hitchcock | *Stories for Late at Night* |
| Holt | *Mistress of Mellyn* |
| Lane | *Let the Hurricane Roar* |
| Mitchell | *Gone with the Wind* |
| Nathan | *Portrait of Jennie* |
| Smith | *Joy in the Morning* |
| Thane | *Tryst* |
| Trahey | *Life with Mother Superior* |
| Weastheimer | *My Sweet Charlie* |

## C. Adult Titles for Good Readers

| Angelou | *I Know Why the Caged Bird Sings* |
|---------|-----------------------------------|
| Borland | *When the Legends Die* |
| Braithwaite | *To Sir, with Love* |
| Brown | *Bury My Heart at Wounded Knee* |
| Brown | *Manchild in the Promised Land* |

| Buck | *The Good Earth* |
| Cleaver | *Soul On Ice* |
| Dunning, ed. | *Reflections on a Gift of Watermelon Pickles* |
| Gaines | *The Autobiography of Miss Jane Pittman* |
| Golding | *Lord of the Flies* |
| Guthrie | *The Big Sky* |
| Hart | *Act One* |
| Kaufman | *Up the Down Staircase* |
| Knowles | *A Separate Peace* |
| Lee | *To Kill a Mockingbird* |
| Little | *The Autobiography of Malcolm X* |
| Massie | *Nicholas and Alexandra* |
| Parks | *A Choice of Weapons* |
| Paton | *Cry the Beloved Country* |
| Remarque | *All Quiet on the Western Front* |
| Rosten | *The Education of Hyman Kaplan* |
| Salinger | *The Catcher in the Rye* |
| Segal | *Love Story* |
| Seton | *Katherine* |
| Smith | *A Tree Grows in Brooklyn* |
| Wouk | *The Caine Mutiny* |
| Wright | *Black Boy* |

## D. Advanced Reading

| Baldwin | *Go Tell It on the Mountain* |
| Camus | *The Plague* |
| Dostoevski | *Crime and Punishment* |
| Dreiser | *An American Tragedy* |
| Faulkner | *The Sound and the Fury* |
| Fitzgerald | *The Great Gatsby* |
| Hemingway | *A Farewell to Arms* |
| Huxley | *Brave New World* |
| Joyce | *Portrait of the Artist as a Young Man* |
| Kafka | *The Trial* |
| Koestler | *Darkness at Noon* |
| Malamud | *The Fixer* |
| Maugham | *Of Human Bondage* |
| Orwell | *1984* |
| Renault | *The King Must Die* |
| Solzhenitsyn | *One Day in the Life of Ivan Denisovitch* |
| Steinbeck | *The Grapes of Wrath* |
| Steinbeck | *Of Mice and Men* |

| Styron | *The Confessions of Nat Turner* |
|--------|--------------------------------|
| Tolstoy | *Anna Karenina* |
| Tolstoy | *War and Peace* |

## A BIBLIOGRAPHY FOR THE LIBRARIAN
## WORKING WITH TEENAGERS

[See Appendix C for a bibliography for young adult librarians prepared by Patty Campbell for this edition.]

# APPENDIX B

# Selection Policies for Books for Young Adults

It is the aim of this library's service to young adults to help them through books to find self-realization, to live in their communities as citizens of this democracy, and to be at home in the world. This aim is constantly kept in mind when books are selected for the young adult collections throughout the system, and each book purchased fits into this plan. The Book Selection Policies for young adult work in this library are based on the following principles:

1. That the young adult collections should be composed of books that widen the boundaries of adolescents' thinking, that enrich their life, and help them fulfill their recreational and emotional needs. Materials to help an adolescent prepare school assignments are in the reference and general adult collections rather than the young adult collections. However, school demands are considered if the books requested are both of a recreational nature and in the field of special interest to teenagers, such as World War I, popular science, etc.

2. That while our aims are clearly stated, the rules for selection cannot be written out ahead of time except in general terms, for each book must be considered separately. In other words, books have both faults and virtues, and if the virtues far overbalance a fault, a book may be included. With this in mind, the so called "touchy" areas in book

This statement of policies was prepared by Margaret Edwards for Enoch Pratt Free Library in 1962. *Ed.*

selection for teenagers are handled as follows: (a) The use of profanity or of frankness in dealing with sex may be deplorable, but when a book opens a clearer vision of life, develops understanding of other people, or breaks down intolerance, these virtues must be weighed against the possible harm to be done by some regrettable word or passage in the book, particularly where taste rather than morals is offended. (b) Simple books of sex information for teenagers belong on the open shelves of young adult collections. It seems important that young adults gain sound information since they are sure to gain information of some kind on the subject. If the books are treated as are interesting books on other subjects, much can be done to give teenagers a healthful attitude toward sex. (c) Religious books of an obviously denominational nature whose primary purpose is to present one sect as superior to another are not purchased for young adult collections, nor are books that belittle any faith. Only well-written books that make no attempt to sway the emotions of the adolescent toward or against any one faith should be included in special collections for young adults.

3. That all types of readers must be considered in setting up a book collection. Simple teenage stories of boy-girl relationships teach young and reluctant readers a love of reading—the first step in the development of any reader. At the other end of the scale is the older, better reader, often the superior student, who is forming his own philosophy and wishes to read adult titles that throw a clear light on the process of living. As the young adult collection serves primarily as an introduction to adult reading, in this library the majority of titles purchased are duplicates of adult books. However, this collection also includes titles written specifically for "teenagers" which are not bought in adult departments. When new titles of this type appear, if there is any question of the age level to which they will appeal, the Coordinators of Work with Children and Young Adults usually agree arbitrarily to place them in one department or the other. Only outstanding titles of books in unusual demand are placed in both the children's and young adult collections.

4. All fiction is read before purchase; also nonfiction titles of biography, travel, humor, drama, etc. Factual books, such as vocational books or those on sport techniques are examined closely. If adult titles recommended for "Y" purchase are not in the Central adult collection, the subject department head concerned is consulted, since the adult department must purchase the first copy of the title or *agree to its addition in the "Y" collection only.* In case of difference of opinion, the Assistant Director or Director is consulted. This applies only to adult titles. Books written specifically for young adults may be purchased even though not in the adult subject department collections.

5. That the young adult librarians working in committees should, after a period of training, be responsible for the selection of new books, but that any book selected may be challenged by any of the young adult librarians at any time, when the book will be reconsidered by the entire group. Though, as a rule, the young adult librarians read the controversial books under consideration and decide by vote in their regular monthly meeting whether to accept or reject these titles, it is the Coordinator of Work with Young Adults who has the final responsibility for and the final authority in the selection of books for young adult collections, subject to the ultimate responsibility of the Director.

6. That when the demand for books on any subject has been fairly met, new books in the field may be rejected, for no other reason except that a wiser use can be made of the book fund. At all times, a new book must be measured against other books available to determine what purchase seems wisest in view of our needs and the funds on hand.

7. That the young adult collection at Central should contain a copy of any book bought for young adults anywhere else in the system, but each branch collection should be made up of the books best suited to the community of young adults it serves.

## APPENDIX C

# A Bibliography
# for the Librarian
# Working with Teenagers
by Patty Campbell

### YOUNG ADULT SERVICES

American Association of School Librarians and the Association for Educational Communications and Technology. *Information Power: Guidelines for School Library Media Programs.* Chicago: ALA; Washington D.C.: AECT, 1988.

American Library Association. Young Adult Library Services Association. *Directions for Library Service to Young Adults.* 2nd ed. Chicago: ALA, 1993.

American Library Association. Young Adult Library Services Association. *Youth Participation in Libraries: A Training Manual.* Chicago: ALA, 1989.

Bodart, Joni Richards, ed. *Booktalk!* New York: H. W. Wilson Co., 1980.

—— *Booktalk! 2.* New York: H. W. Wilson Co., 1985.

—— *Booktalk! 3.* New York: H. W. Wilson Co., 1988.

—— *Booktalk! 4.* New York: H. W. Wilson Co., 1992.

Broderick, Dorothy, ed. *The VOYA Reader.* Metuchen, N.J.: Scarecrow, 1990.

Chelton, Mary K. and James M. Rosinia. *Bare Bones: Young Adult Services Tips for Public Library Generalists.* Chicago: YALSA/PLA/ALA, 1993.

Farmer, Lesley S. J. *Young Adult Services in the Small Library.* Chicago: ALA, 1992.

Jones, Patrick. *Connecting Young Adults and Libraries: A How-to-Do-It Manual.* How-to-Do-It-Manuals for Libraries, no. 19. New York: Neal-Schuman, 1992.

Rochman, Hazel. *Tales of Love and Terror: Booktalking the Classics, Old and New.* Chicago: ALA, 1987.

Shaevel, Evelyn and Peggy O'Donnell. *Courtly Love in the Shopping Mall: Humanities Programming for Young Adults.* Chicago: ALA, 1991.

Weiner, J. Pamela and Ruth Stein. *Adolescents, Literature, and Work with Youth.* New York: Haworth, 1985.


## YOUNG ADULT LITERATURE—BACKGROUND AND COLLECTION ASSESSMENT

American Library Association. Young Adult Services Division. *Hit List: Frequently Challenged Young Adult Titles.* Chicago: ALA, 1989.

Carter, Betty and Richard F. Abrahamson. *Nonfiction for Young Adults: From Delight to Wisdom.* Phoenix: Oryx, 1990.

Cline, Ruth and William McBride. *A Guide to Literature for Young Adults.* Glenview, Ill.: Scott, Foresman, 1983.

Cuseo, Allan. *Homosexual Characters in YA Novels: A Literary Analysis, 1969–1982.* Metuchen, N.J.: Scarecrow, 1992.

Donelson, Kenneth L. and Alleen Pace Nilsen. *Literature for Today's Young Adults.* 4th ed. New York: HarperCollins, 1993.

Gallant, Jennifer Jung. *Best Videos for Children and Young Adults.* Santa Barbara, Calif.: ABC-Clio, 1990.

Gallo, Donald R., ed. *Literature for Teenagers: New Books, New Approaches.* The Connecticut Council of Teachers of English, 1993.

Rochman, Hazel. *Against Borders: Promoting Books for a Multicultural World.* Chicago: ALA, 1993.

Rosenberg, Betty and Diana Tixier Herald. *Genreflecting: A Guide to Reading Interests in Genre Fiction.* 3rd ed. Englewood, Colo.: Libraries Unlimited, 1991.

Schon, Isabel. *Books in Spanish for Children and Young Adults.* Metuchen, N.J.: Scarecrow, 1989.

Spencer, Pamela. *What Do Young Adults Read Next?* Detroit: Gale, 1993.

Zvirin, Stephanie. *The Best Years of Their Lives: A Resource Guide for Teenagers in Crisis.* Chicago: ALA, 1992.

*Young Adult Literature—Background and Collection Assessment—Book Lists*

American Library Association. Young Adult Services Division. *Genre Lists and Tip Kits.* (Horror, science fiction, romance, humor, mystery, fantasy, sports; includes bookmarks and stickers) Chicago: ALA, 1991.

American Library Association. Young Adult Services Division. *Nothin' But the Best: Best of the Best Books for Young Adults 1966–1986.* Chicago: ALA, 1987.

American Library Association. Young Adult Services Division. *Outstanding Books for the College Bound.* (Five brochures: Fiction, Nonfiction, Biography, Fine Arts, Theater) Chicago: ALA, 1990.

Bodart, Joni. *One Hundred World Class Thin Books, or What to Read When Your Book Report Is Due Tomorrow!* Englewood, Colo.: Libraries Unlimited, 1993.

*Books for You: A Booklist for Senior High Students.* Shirley Wurth, ed. 11th ed. Urbana, Ill.: National Council of Teachers of English, 1992.

*Junior High School Library Catalog.* 6th ed. New York: H. W. Wilson, 1990.

Kies, Cosette. *Supernatural Fiction for Teens.* 2nd ed. Englewood, Colo.: Libraries Unlimited, 1992.

*Senior High School Library Catalog.* 14th ed. New York: H. W. Wilson, 1990.

*Your Reading: A Booklist for Junior High and Middle School Students.* Alleen Pace Nilsen, ed. 8th ed. Urbana, Ill.: National Council of Teachers of English, 1991.

YOUNG ADULT LITERATURE—BIOGRAPHICAL RESOURCES

*Authors and Artists for Young Adults.* Agnes Garrett and Helga P. McCue, eds. vol. 1– . Detroit, Mich.: Gale, 1989– .

Gallo, Donald, comp. and ed. *Speaking for Ourselves: Autobiographical Sketches by Notable Authors of Books for Young Adults.* Urbana, Ill.: National Council of Teachers of English, 1990.

Gallo, Donald, comp. and ed. *Speaking for Ourselves, Too: More Autobiographical Sketches by Notable Authors of Books for Young Adults.* Urbana, Ill.: National Council of Teachers of English, 1993.

Twayne Young Adult Author Series. Patricia J. Campbell, ed. New York: Twayne Publishers, 1985– .

*Twentieth Century Young Adult Writers.* Laura Standley Berger, ed. Detroit, Mich.: St. James Pr., 1994.

## PROFESSIONAL AND REVIEW MAGAZINES

*ALAN Review.* Urbana, Ill.: NCTE.

*Appraisal: Science Books for Young People.* Boston: Boston University School of Education.

*Book Links.* Chicago: ALA.

*Book Report.* Worthington, Ohio: Linworth Publishing.

*Booklist.* Chicago: ALA.

*Bulletin of the Center for Children's Books.* Chicago, University of Chicago.

*Emergency Librarian.* London, Ontario: Dyad Services.

*English Journal.* Urbana, Ill.: NCTE.

*Horn Book.* ("The Sand in the Oyster" column) Boston: Horn Book.

*Horn Book Guide.* Boston: Horn Book.

*Interracial Books for Children Bulletin.* New York: Council on Interracial Books for Children.

*Journal of Reading.* Newark, Del.: International Reading Assn.

*Journal of Youth Services.* Chicago: ALA.

*Kliatt Young Adult Paperback Book Guide.* Newton, Mass.: Kliatt.

*School Library Journal.* New York: Bowker.

*School Library Media Quarterly.* Chicago, ALA.

*Signal.* Newark, Del.: International Reading Association.

*Voice of Youth Advocates.* Metuchen, N.J.: Scarecrow.

*Wilson Library Bulletin* ("Young Adult Perplex," "Middle Readers," and "School Media Matters" columns) New York: H. W. Wilson.

## JOURNAL ARTICLES BY MARGARET EDWARDS

### *Alexander, Margaret (maiden name)*

"Introducing Books to Young Readers." *ALA Bulletin* 32 (1 October 1938):685–90.

"How to Read and Like It: A Discussion of the Poorer Reader." *Pennsylvania Library and Museum Notes* 17 (July 1939):2–6.

"Promotion of Recreational Reading for Young People." *Pennsylvania Library and Museum Notes* 18 (April 1941):11–17.

"Wisdom Crying in the Streets." *Library Journal* 68 (1 May 1943):347–49.

"Adventures with a Book Wagon." *Illinois Libraries* 26 (April 1944):132–37.

*Edwards, Margaret Alexander*

"Introducing Books to Young Readers." In ALA, Libraries for Children and Young People Division, Post-War Planning Committee, *The Public Library Plans for the Teen Age.* Chicago: ALA, 1948, 57–62.

"The Librarian and the United Nations Youth." *Top of the News* 4 (September 1948):14–17.

"Future with Young People." *Iowa Library Quarterly* 16 (April 1951):131–38.

"Service to Young Adults at the Enoch Pratt Free Library." *Indiana Librarian* 10 (September 1955):56–59; Library Journal 82 (15 September 1957):2170.

"Service for the Adolescent." *Top of the News* 12 (December 1955):35–37.

"A Little Learnin'; Satin Gowns in Childress, Texas." *ALA Bulletin* 50 (June 1956):379–86.

"Many a Thousand Brick." *Library Journal* 81 (15 May 1956):1282–85.

"Mrs. Grundy, Go Home." *Wilson Library Bulletin* 33 (December 1958):304–5.

"Introducing Young People to a Life-long Pleasure." *Library Journal* 83 (15 January 1960):218–21.

"Open Wonderful New Worlds." *Wilson Library Bulletin* 34 (March 1960):494–95.

"It All Started with Prometheus." *California Librarian* 21 (April 1960):93–96.

"Book Selection for Young Adults." School Library Association, California *Bulletin* 31 (May 1960):9–11.

"Time When It's Best to Read and Let Read." *Wilson Library Bulletin* 35 (September 1960):43–45.

[Review of] ALA, AASL. Discussion Guide for Use with the Standards. *School Library Journal* 10 (January 1961):44–45.

"For Auld Lang Syne, My Dears." *Maryland Libraries* 27 (Winter 1961):11–13.

"In the Opinion of Teenagers." *Top of the News* 18 (December 1961):57–60; (March 1962):72–73; 19 (October 1962):67–68.

"How to Give a Book Talk." *Ohio Library Association Bulletin* 33 (April 1963):21–23.

"The Librarian, the Teen-ager and the Book." *Florida Libraries* 14 (June 1963):11–13.

"Taming the Young Barbarian." *Library Journal* 89 (15 April 1964):1819–21.

"Art of Librarianship." *Southeastern Librarian* 14 (Summer 1964):114–19.

"Book Is to Read." *Idaho Librarian* 16 (July 1964):97–103.

"Time and Season for the Better Reader." *Top of the News* 21 (April 1965):229–35.

"The Fair Garden and the Swarm of Beasts." *Library Journal* (1 September 1965):3379–83.

"A Long Way to Tipperary." In *The Library Reaches Out,* ed. K. M. Coplan and E. Castagna. Dobbs Ferry, N.Y.: Oceana, 1965.

"City Kid and the Library." *Top of the News* 24 (November 1967):62–71.

"Urban Library and the Adolescent." *Library Quarterly* 38 (January 1968):70–77.

"YA: The Library Bastard." *Utah Libraries* 12 (Spring 1969):32–43.

"Ladder to Lean on the Sky." *Catholic Library World* 42 (November 1970):161–67.

"Youth, Books, and Guidance." *North Carolina Libraries* 28 (Winter 1970):8–14.

"No Barefeet." In *Survival Kit.* Chicago: ALA, 1971.

"Where's Nicholas Vedder?" *Canadian Library Journal* 28 (September 1971):371–73.

"I Once Did See Joe Wheeler Plain." *Junior Library History* 6 (October 1971):291–302.

"Public Library and Young Adults: A Viewpoint." In *Educating the Library User,* ed. J. Lubans. New York: Bowker, 1974, 56–58.

"Reason to Read." *Canadian Library Journal* 31 (August 1974):307–8.

# Notes and References

## Chapter I

1. Octavius Walton, *Whiter than Snow*. One of a series of religious tracts published at the turn of the century.

2. "If you have two loaves of bread, sell one and buy a hyacinth," saying attributed variously to Persian, Greek, or Chinese tradition. Yet another version appears in *Not by Bread Alone* by James Terry White (1907).

3. Rebecca Sophia Clarke (Sophie May, pseud.), *Little Prudy* (1909). One of a series that includes *Little Prudy's Dotty Dimple, Little Prudy's Sister Susie, Little Prudy's Cousin Grace*, etc.; Annie Fellows Johnston, *The Little Colonel* series (1901–1909); Harriet Milford Lothrop (Margaret Sidney, pseud.), *The Five Little Peppers* series (around 1880); Eleanor Porter, *Pollyanna* (1913); Lucy Maud Montgomery, *Anne of Green Gables* (1908).

4. Horatio Alger, *A Boy's Fortune*. One of a series of romantic fantasies (1869–1890) about the rise to fame and fortune of disadvantaged boys through hard work and pluck.

5. Mary Jane (Hawes) Holmes, Meadow Brook Farm series (late nineteenth century).

6. Hans and Fritz were characters in a long-lived and popular comic strip created by Rudolph Dirks beginning in 1897, titled "The Captain and the Kids" but better known as "The Katzenjammer Kids"; "Mutt and Jeff" was a comic strip drawn by Bud Fisher; Maggie and Jiggs were characters in a comic strip entitled "Bringing Up Father," created by George MacManus.

7. Klara Mundt (Louise Mulbach, pseud.), *Henry VIII and His Court* (1864).

147

8. "Are not two sparrows sold for a penny? And not one of them will fall to the ground without your Father's will." Matthew 10:29.

## Chapter II

1. Maureen Daly, *Seventeenth Summer* (1942); "Ken McLaughlin": An exhaustive search by Los Angeles Public Library has failed to locate a source for this character; Jody Baxter, a character in *The Yearling* by Marjorie Kinnan Rawlings (1938); Holden Caulfield, a character in *Catcher in the Rye* by J. D. Salinger (1951); Dobie Gillis, a character in *The Many Loves of Dobie Gillis* by Max Shulman (1951). Later also a character in a television series; Jessamyn West, *Cress Delahanty* (1953).

2. "Chinese girl," in *The Good Earth* by Pearl Buck (1931); "A German boy," in *All Quiet on the Western Front* by Erich Maria Remarque (1929); "A Zulu father," in *Cry the Beloved Country* by Alan Paton (1948).

3. Benedict Freedman and Nancy Freedman, *Mrs. Mike* (1947).

4. Henry Gregor Felsen, *Hot Rod* (1950).

5. "The ruler of the Queen's navee," a line from an aria sung by the pompous Sir Joseph Porter, K.C.B., First Lord of the Admiralty, in Gilbert and Sullivan's light opera *Pinafore*.

6. Dr. Benjamin Spock, pediatrician and social activist renowned for his book of many editions, *Baby and Child Care*, first published in 1946.

7. Anna Curry, who later became director of the Pratt Library.

8. David Eli Lilienthal, widely respected U.S. statesman and chair of the Atomic Energy Commission 1946–1950.

## Chapter III

1. The offer was made by Harold Hamill, former assistant director at the Pratt Library, then head of Kansas City Public Library.

2. The article was "Adult Books for Teen-agers," *Library Journal* 75 (15 October 1950):1765–73.

3. The article was "Wisdom Crying in the Streets," *Library Journal* 68 (1 May 1943):347–49.

4. Kathleen Norris, popular and prolific romance novelist in the 1940s, wife of writer Frank Norris, and author of *Hearbroken Melody, Mother, The Sea Gull, Sisters,* and others; Zane Grey, popular and prolific writer of westerns.

5. Wendell Wilkie, *One World* (1942) (U.S. presidential candidate in the election of 1944).

## Chapter IV

1. Obviously, Edwards uses the adjective "gay" in this sentence not to indicate homosexuality but in the sense of "cheerful, carefree."

2. Dwight Lyman Moody (1837–1899), popular and influential evangelist, and Ira D. Sankey (1840–1908), evangelist, organist and singer, who traveled and performed with Moody.

## Chapter V

1. Betty Smith, *A Tree Grows in Brooklyn* (1943); Pearl Buck, *The Good Earth* (1931); John Hersey, *Hiroshima* (1946); Erich Maria Remarque, *All Quiet on the Western Front* (1929); Claude Brown, *Manchild in the Promised Land* (1965).

2. Somerset Maugham, *Of Human Bondage* (1915); Emily Bronte, *Wuthering Heights* (1847); Nicholas Monsarrat, *The Cruel Sea* (1951); Irving Stone, *Love Is Eternal* (1954); Mildred Walker, *Winter Wheat* (1944); Margaret Mitchell, *Gone with the Wind* (1936); Gwen Terasaki, *Bridge to the Sun* (1957); Agnes Keith, *Three Came Home* (1947).

3. Clifton Fadiman, literary critic and popularizer of reading and well-known radio and television master-of-ceremonies in the 1950s. Author of *The Lifetime Reading Plan* (1960).

4. "Ouida" was the pseudonym of Louise de la Ramee (1839–1908), and author of *A Dog of Flanders* (1863); also *Moths, In a Winter City, Chandos, Bebee,* and others.

5. Jesse Stuart, author of *The Beatinest Boy* (1953), *The Good Spirit of Laurel Ridge* (1953), *Red Mule* (1955), and others.

6. Although the term *Communistic* here is meant jocularly, the year 1957, when this was written, was the height of the anti-communist sentiment stirred up by Senator Joseph McCarthy's investigations.

## Chapter VI

1. From "Excelsior!", a poem by Henry Wadsworth Longfellow (1842), in which a young man persists in climbing a mountain, only to be found frozen to death at the pinnacle, a banner with the strange device, "Excelsior!" clutched in his hand.

2. John Erskine (1879–1951), scholar, teacher, and musician, taught at Columbia University from 1909 to 1937, initiated Great Books courses for undergraduates, co-edited *The Cambridge History of American Literature* and authored *The Private Life of Helen of Troy.*

3. Mary Lee Bundy, *Metropolitan Public Library Users: A Report of a Survey of Adult Library Use in the Maryland-Baltimore-Washington Metropolitan Area* (School of Library and Information Services, University of Maryland, 1968).

4. Morris Raphael Cohen, professor of philosophy emeritus at University of Chicago in 1938.

5. Lawrence Mervil Tibbett (1896–1960), popular American operatic baritone who sang on stage, radio, and in the movies.

6. "The medium is the message" is a much-quoted statement by Marshall McLuhan meaning that "the form of a message determines the way in which

that message will be perceived, and, additionally, that the means of communication have a greater influence on people than the information it carries." (*Dictionary of Cultural Literacy*, 128)

7. VISTA (Volunteers in Service to America) was a domestic Peace Corps-style federal agency during the War on Poverty in the 1960s.

8. The list of 1963 bestsellers by *Publishers Weekly* included *Happiness Is a Warm Puppy* and *Security Is a Thumb and a Blanket*, both by Charles Schulz; *Profiles in Courage* by John F. Kennedy; *O Ye Jigs and Juleps!* by Virginia Carey Hudson; and *I Owe Russia $1200* by Bob Hope.

9. Everett R. Perry, vice-president of the American Library Association, 1930.

10. Agnes Keith, author of *Three Came Home* (1947), *Land Below the Wind* (1939), *Beloved Exiles* (1972), and *Bare Feet in the Palace* (1955).

11. Leo Rosten, *The Education of Hyman Kaplan* (1937); Clarence Day, *Life with Father* (1935).

12. Lowell A. Martin, *Students and the Pratt Library: Challenge and Opportunity*, Deiches Fund Studies of Public Library Service, no. 1 (Baltimore: Enoch Pratt Free Library, 1963).

13. "Lamb's character," in "On Eating Roast Pig," a much-anthologized essay by Charles Lamb (1775–1834) that makes the point that it is not necessary to burn down the whole house to have roast pork.

14. George Orwell, *1984* (1950); William Golding, *Lord of the Flies* (1959); John H. Griffin, *Black like Me* (1961).

## Chapter VII

1. In 1971 the ALA Placement Center reported 2.17 applicants for each job opening; by 1974 there were nearly 5 (Margaret Myers, "The Job Market for Librarians," *Library Trends*, Spring 1986, 646).

2. W. H. Webb, "Will the Resources Head Wag the Imperative Tail?" Carnegie Commission on Higher Education Report, *College and Research Libraries* 33(July 1972):269–70.

## Chapter VIII

1. The incidents mentioned here were written about in *A Tree Grows in Brooklyn* by Betty Smith; *The Sound and the Fury* by William Faulkner; *The Human Comedy* by William Saroyan; and *Black Boy* by Richard Wright.

# Index